The Selected Poems of
YVOR WINTERS

*This book was supported by a grant
from the Eric Mathieu King Fund of
The Academy of American Poets*

The Selected Poems of
YVOR WINTERS

Edited by R. L. Barth

Introduction by Helen Pinkerton Trimpi

SWALLOW PRESS/OHIO UNIVERSITY PRESS
ATHENS

Swallow Press / Ohio University Press, Athens, Ohio 45701
© 1999 by Janet Lewis Winters
Introduction © 1999 by Helen Pinkerton Trimpi
© 1931, 1934, 1943, 1950, 1952, 1960, 1966 by Yvor Winters
© 1937, 1943 by New Directions Publishing Company

Swallow Press / Ohio University Press books
are printed on acid-free paper ⊗ ™

03 02 01 00 99   5 4 3 2 1

*Cover photograph of Yvor Winters in the Santa Fe Canyon
(1920s) from the Winters family album.*

Library of Congress Cataloging-in-Publication Data
Winters, Yvor, 1900–1968.
[Poems. Selections]
The selected poems of Yvor Winters / edited by R. L. Barth ;
introduction by Helen Pinkerton Trimpi.
p.   cm.
Includes bibliographical references and index.
ISBN 0-8040-1012-9 (cloth : alk. paper). — ISBN 0-8040-1013-7
(pbk. alk. paper)
I. Barth, R. L. (Robert L.) II. Title.
PS3545.I765A6 1999
811'.52—dc21   98-49855
                                                                   CIP

The Dedication

To J.L.W.

Confusion, cold and still,
Impeding act and thought,
And the inchoate will;
With these at last I wrought.

Concentered with your mind,
My vision then grew just:
When I no point can find,
I wait, because I must.

Hard study eats to age.
These words are few to show:
I leave them on the page,
Though you alone will know.

Contents

Acknowledgments

That many people helped me as I edited this book goes, I hope, without saying; and it is a pleasure to acknowledge their acts of kindness and assistance. Janet Lewis Winters allowed this book to happen; and Dan and Nancy Winters were always willing to answer my questions and talk about Yvor Winters more generally, as well as reading parts of my manuscript. Dan has also aided my work materially, checking the family archives, providing dates, sources, and manuscripts. Jeff Akard, Turner Cassity, the late Charles Gullans, Helen Pinkerton Trimpi, and Thomas Zaniello, who first introduced me to the writings of Yvor Winters nearly thirty years ago, have over the years taught me a good deal about the critic, poet, and man. Timothy Steele, both by the example of his edition of the poems of J. V. Cunningham and by answering many of my questions about his editorial work, certainly made my work less bewildering. Grosvenor Powell gave me most of the papers relating to his bibliography of Yvor Winters, and I consulted them frequently. I would also like to thank James Cummins, Timothy Quinn, and John Rettig. The cover photograph of Yvor Winters in the Santa Fe Canyon (1920s) is from the Winters family album, obtained through the kind offices of Margaret M. Furbush, to whom I am grateful—as to Janet Lewis Winters for allowing me to use it. I am grateful to David Sanders, the director of the Ohio University Press/Swallow Press, for suggesting this book and remaining unflappable when the original manuscript was lost to a burned out computer. Finally, I would like to thank my wife, Susan, conventionally for the inevitable patience but also for tracking down and checking out books from the library, and my daughter, Ann, who let me borrow her editions of Catullus.

Obviously, any errors of judgment or of fact are my own responsibility.

R.L.B.

For insights, admonitions (not all accepted) and encouragement I have most valued the conversation, in Palo Alto and Edmonton, of Christopher Drummond. Stellar teacher and critic, he reads English poetry with a sharper and more inspired eye than anyone I have known except Winters. For a helpful reading of my essay I wish to thank Timothy Steele, whose judicious introduction to *The Poems of J. V. Cunningham* (Ohio Univ. Press/Swallow Press, 1997) I recommend to all lovers of the short poem. Janet Lewis Winters, now ninety-eight and friend of more than fifty years, listened to the essay and confirmed many details. Other acknowledgments are made through references in the body of the text.

H.P.T.

Preface

Although better known as a critic, Yvor Winters created a body of excellent poetry that deserves to be more widely known than it has been. For this reason, as well as for the more practical reason that his poetry is, as I write, out of print, a new edition of the work is imperative.

The main body of Winters's poetry was collected in two volumes during his lifetime: *Collected Poems* (1952; rev. ed. 1960) and *The Early Poems of Yvor Winters 1920–1928* (1966). For Winters, the former volume represented his more important achievement; it "contains everything which I wish to keep" ([6]). *The Early Poems*, on the other hand, served as a preemptive strike: "I publish this book to provide an authorized edition of my early and 'experimental' work. Some one would do this in any event, and probably some one who would sweep all of my uncollected work into a single volume, with no indication of what I had considered my best work as I was writing and publishing it" (7). This statement does not mean he placed little value on the early poems. On the contrary, he said, "I wish to be clear on two points: I regard this work as inferior to my later work; I regard it as very good of its kind, quite as good as any of the 'experimental' work of this century" (7–8). Nevertheless, Winters collected only a relatively small number of the early poems. One reason is indicated above: he considered the early poems inferior to his later, metrical poetry. There is another reason, too. Winters wanted the *Collected Poems* to "represent . . . a kind of definition by example of the style which I have been trying to achieve for a matter of thirty years" ([6]). Characteristically, he wanted to provide a map of his achievement, deleting all potential distractions and dead ends.

There is certainly nothing wrong with Winters's rationale. Indeed, it makes perfect sense. However, my belief in editing a volume of selected poems arranged chronologically is that the style will necessarily be defined along the way and that, furthermore, some of the stylistic distractions and dead ends are inherently interesting, adding to a complete view of Winters's achievement. Frankly, too many fine poems were passed over in the *Collected Poems*. Like Winters, I believe the later poems represent the finer achievement, but I also think it would be a shame as well as a distortion to cut back too severely the early poems. Thus, my selection is more generous than the *Collected Poems* with the early "experimental" poems and less so with the later poems.

Although I have consulted Winters's individual collections, with the exceptions recorded in the notes I have used the *Collected Poems* and the *Early Poems* for my texts. Winters rewrote some of the early poems that he included in the *Collected Poems* without noting the fact. In some cases his revisions amounted to little more than tinkering with punctuation. In other cases, however, he rewrote so radically as to produce different poems. I am aware that many of the revisions appeared as early as the *Poems* (1940). I am also aware that some of the transitional and later poems were revised—though, except for "The Fable," none too radically—but they always appeared together as an integral part of Winters's body of poetry, from *Poems* to the two editions of the *Collected Poems*. That is, the transitional poems were never singled out for a separate edition. The editorial question is whether mixing early poems later revised with early poems untouched is distorting. I believe it is. Therefore, I have used the *Early Poems* as my source for the poetry through 1928—that is, the poems up to and including "Simplex Munditiis" in this edition.

As I noted, the poems in this edition are arranged more or less chronologically by individual book appearance. The main exception is "The Dedication," with which Winters prefaced *Before Disaster* (1934). The poems from "Two Songs of Advent" to "Alone" first appeared in *The Immobile Wind* (1921); the poems from "Winter Echo" to "A Deer" first appeared in *The Magpie's Shadow* (1922); the poems from "The Precincts of February" to "Prayer beside a Lamp" first appeared in *The Bare Hills* (1927); "Vacant Lot" and "The Deep" appeared as part of "Fire Sequence" in the *American Caravan* (1927), the former remaining uncollected in book form until *The Early Poems* but the latter appearing in *The Proof* (1930); "Demigod" remained uncollected until *The Uncollected Poems of Yvor Winters 1919–1928*

(1997); the poems from "Orange Tree" to "For Howard Baker" first appeared in *The Proof* (Winters's transitional book); the poems from "The Slow Pacific Swell" to "A Vision" first appeared in *The Journey and Other Poems* (1931); the poems from "Anacreontic" to "Chiron," "A Leave-Taking" excepted, first appeared in *Before Disaster*; "A Leave-Taking" and the poems from "Heracles" to "On the Portrait of a Scholar of the Italian Renaissance" first appeared in *Poems*, although some had previously appeared in the anthology *Twelve Poets of the Pacific*, edited by Winters; the poems from "A Winter Evening" to "Moonlight Alert," "At the Site of the Murphy Cabin" excepted, first appeared in *The Giant Weapon* (1943); "At the Site of the Murphy Cabin" remained uncollected until *The Uncollected Poems of Yvor Winters 1929–1957* (1997); "To the Holy Spirit" and "A Song in Passing" first appeared in *Three Poems* (1950); "At the San Francisco Airport" first appeared in the *Collected Poems* (1960); and "To Herbert Dean Meritt" appeared in a Winters book first in *The Collected Poetry of Yvor Winters*. A bibliography of Winters's books of poetry precedes the notes for the reader interested in publication details.

R. L. Barth

Introduction

Yvor Winters as Critic and Poet

Biographical Introduction

> Our finely grained identities
> Are but this golden sediment.
>
> *("On the Portrait of a Scholar of the Italian Renaissance")*

The American poet and critic Arthur Yvor Winters was born in Chicago on October 17, 1900, son of Harry Lewis Winters and Faith Evangeline Ahnefeldt Winters. His father, after working in real estate, became a grain and stock trader on the Chicago Stock Exchange. Although Winters lived briefly in Seattle and visited grandparents in the Pasadena area as a child, Chicago was his home until 1919. After education at Evanston and Nicholas Senn High Schools, he attended the University of Chicago for four quarters, 1917–18. There he studied science but also became a member of the Poetry Club, to which belonged the young writers Monroe Wheeler, later director of exhibitions at the Museum of Modern Art in New York; Glenway Wescott, poet and novelist; Elizabeth Madox Roberts, poet and novelist; Pearl Andelson Sherry; and Maurice Lesemann, later a businessman. He had already begun his lifelong reading and writing of poetry in high school, but expanded his activity through a friendship with Harriet Monroe, founder and editor of *Poetry: A Magazine of Verse*.

Winters's life abruptly changed when, in the winter of 1918–19, he was diagnosed with tuberculosis. He was sent first to Riverside, California, then to St. Vincent's Sanatorium and later Sunmount Sanatorium in Santa Fe, New Mexico, for treatment. For the next five years his career was shaped by the need to recuperate from his illness. While at Sunmount, he met Marsden Hartley, the Modernist painter. Of one of Hartley's New Mexico landscapes Winters wrote that it possessed an "ominous physical mysticism," which Winters himself felt was "the principal characteristic of this country." His poetry from this early period in *The Immobile Wind* (1921) and *The*

Magpie's Shadow (1922) clearly reflects not only the hallucinatory quality he sensed in the landscape but the isolation and enforced physical repose that treatment of tuberculosis at the time required. In later years he wrote of the enervation the disease induced: "The disease filled the body with a fatigue so heavy that it was an acute pain, pervasive and poisonous" (Brigitte Hoy Carnochan, *The Strength of Art: Poets and Poetry in the Lives of Yvor Winters and Janet Lewis* [Stanford Univ. Libraries, 1984], 11–17).

Released from Sunmount in October 1921, he taught for two years in high schools in the coal mining camps of Cerillos and Madrid, New Mexico, experience which forms the background for many of his early poems included here. At this time Janet Lewis, who had joined the Poetry Club in Chicago, was diagnosed with the same illness, and came to Sunmount in 1922, where they met and formed a friendship that resulted in their engagement and marriage on June 22, 1926.

Meanwhile, Winters had resumed his college education by enrolling at the University of Colorado at Boulder, where in nine successive quarters, 1923–25, he achieved his B.A. and M.A. in Romance Languages and Phi Beta Kappa membership. With degrees in hand, he accepted a teaching job at the University of Idaho, Moscow, which he held for two winters, 1925–27. Some of his experiences on a four-day train journey from Boulder to Moscow are reflected in his poem "The Journey." The period spent teaching in Moscow, living with his two Airedales as a boarder with a local family, forms the background of his only work of fiction, *The Brink of Darkness*, first published in Lincoln Kirstein's distinguished literary journal *Hound & Horn* in 1932. After returning to Santa Fe, he moved with his wife to Palo Alto, California, where he enrolled as a Ph.D. candidate at Stanford University in the fall of 1927.

During the years prior to his move to northern California, while living in Santa Fe, Boulder, and Moscow, Winters had published, besides *The Immobile Wind* and *The Magpie's Shadow*, nearly a dozen reviews in periodicals such as *Poetry*, *Dial*, and *This Quarter*. Of the poems included in the first two books, Brigitte Carnochan writes in *The Strength of Art* that many grew out of experiments in Imagist technique while Winters was at St. Vincent's and Sunmount (17). He also engaged in extensive correspondence not only with his Chicago friends but with other poets and critics in the East, the South, and abroad, including Hart Crane, Allen Tate, and Ezra Pound. He was well known as a modern poet and critic before arriving at Stanford, a fact that affected his career at that institution.

From 1927 to 1935 he was a graduate student and taught as an instructor in the English department. His dissertation concerned modern American literature, which at the time was considered an anomalous subject for scholarly study but was welcomed by the department chairman, William Dinsmore Briggs, a scholar of Renaissance humanism and Ben Jonson. During this period Winters published *The Bare Hills* (1927), *The Proof* (1930), *The Journey and Other Poems* (1931), and *Before Disaster* (1934). In addition, he founded, with Janet Lewis and Howard Baker, a little magazine of poetry and fiction, the *Gyroscope* (May 1929–February 1930), and served as Western editor for *Hound & Horn*, from 1931 to 1934. He continued to publish extensively as a critic. A daughter, Joanna, was born in 1931.

After taking his Ph.D. degree in 1934, Winters remained in the English department, partly for reasons of his and his wife's health, until his retirement in 1966. A son, Daniel, was born in 1938. During World War II Winters applied for military service, was rejected because of his medical history, and served in the Citizens' Defense Corps as Zone Warden for Los Altos. When Richard Foster Jones became department chairman in 1946, he urged Winters's promotion and his supervision of the Creative Writing Fellowships for poetry. During these years he was made a member of the National Institute of Arts and Letters and in 1960 received the Bollingen prize for poetry. He further established his reputation as a poet, through editing *Twelve Poets of the Pacific* (1937), publishing his *Poems* (1940) on his own press and *The Giant Weapon* (1943), editing *Poets of the Pacific: Second Series* (1949), and publishing with Alan Swallow his *Collected Poems* (1952) and *The Early Poems* (1966).

His first three critical books, *Primitivism and Decadence: A Study of American Experimental Poetry* (1937), *Maule's Curse: Seven Studies in the History of American Obscurantism* (1938), and *The Anatomy of Nonsense* (1943), were collected with an additional essay in *In Defense of Reason* and published by Alan Swallow in 1947. These essays were the work of fifteen years, many growing directly out of his teaching of American literature at Stanford. Winters felt, as he wrote in his preface, that the collection developed a single theory of literature and a single theory of the history of literature since the Renaissance. These were followed by his book *Edwin Arlington Robinson* (1946) and another collection of essays, *The Function of Criticism: Problems and Exercises* (1957). These books, in conjunction with his final critical study, *Forms of Discovery* (1967), and an anthology edited with Kenneth Fields, *Quest for Reality: An Anthology of Short Poems in English* (1969), form a coherent and lucid defense of the kind of poetry that Winters most admired and sought to establish in the English language in the twentieth century.

In 1961 a special issue of *Sequoia* (winter 1961) was dedicated to Winters by friends and former students, and in 1966 the English department published in honor of his retirement a collection of twenty-six poems by friends and students, *Laurel, Archaic, Rude*, edited by myself. After two operations for cancer of the throat, Winters died on January 25, 1968, at Stanford Hospital. In 1973 Francis Murphy edited *Yvor Winters: Uncollected Essays and Reviews* (1973)—an incomplete collection—and Janet Lewis edited *The Collected Poems of Yvor Winters* (1978)—also not entirely complete. In 1981 *Southern Review* published a special issue in his honor edited by Donald E. Stanford. R. L. Barth has since edited and published two books of Winters's uncollected poems, for the periods 1919–1928 and 1929–1957.

Allen Tate, with whom Winters had corresponded in the early years and argued about poetry—with "great zeal"—wrote that of his generation, "he is one of three major poets," and that "an ignorant and superstitious generation has chosen to be unaware" of his "powerful verse" (*Sequoia* [winter 1961]: 2–3). More than twenty years later, on the occasion of an exhibition of the Winters-Lewis Papers at the Stanford Library, United States Foreign Service diplomat Henry Ramsey wrote of the "obsidian-like self-confidence in critical matters" of his friend and the teacher of his youth, and that "Joy to him was experience transformed to language, both mysteries to probe, both joys to encounter with the fullness of one's powers" (*Sequoia* [autumn 1984]: 49).

On the same occasion, the poet Edgar Bowers recalled that

Winters displayed an "egalitarian spirit" in the classroom and out, and that he possessed "no ordinary sense of humor." Bowers defined it as a kind of *hilaritas*, meaning (quoting Dietrich Bonhoeffer) "not only serenity, in the classical sense of the word, such as we find in Raphael and Mozart," but what Bonhoeffer describes "as confidence in their own work, a certain boldness and defiance of the world and of popular opinion, a steadfast certainty that what they are doing will benefit the world, even though it does not approve, a magnificent self-assurance" (*Sequoia* [autumn 1984]: 52–56). Of his classroom method, the poet Thom Gunn remembered that he proceeded "by means of persuasion and demonstration rather than dogmatic assertion, . . . always prepared to discuss the view of the opposition" (*Southern Review* 17 [1981]: 687).

Scott Momaday, poet, novelist, and painter, with whom Winters shared a love of New Mexico, speculated that had he not been a poet, "had he not 'taken literature seriously,' as he put it" to Momaday, he would have been a farmer. "And he would have been, like Jefferson, a farmer of strong philosophical persuasion, a man of original thoughts in any case" (*Strength of Art*, 7). Kenneth Fields, among others, notes that Winters showed "great kindness and generosity toward those who wanted to learn from him" and that "for him literature was a supremely important and exciting endeavor" (*Sequoia* [autumn 1984]: 60).

Of his character, Turner Cassity specified his "granitic integrity" and, of his teaching of the writing of poetry, wrote that "the response to the immediate . . . was his specific genius" (*Southern Review* 17 [1981]: 700, 694). Separate memoirs by poets Kenneth Fields, Philip Levine, Donald Hall, and Donald Davie, and by Winters's colleague in American Literature, David Levin, record Winters's teaching style, his personal generosity, his humor, his fondness for boxing, his love of Airedales, and the egalitarian spirit noted by Bowers. Of his integrity, Levine, in a poem entitled "30," records an illustrative anecdote. While conversing in his garden in Los Altos with Levine (then a poetry fellow at Stanford), Winters, as Levine remembers, said: "'Philip, we must never lie, / or we shall lose our souls'" (*The Bread of Time: Toward an Autobiography* [New York: Knopf, 1994], 256). The quotation indeed illustrates the man.

The Search for Critical Understanding

Constant principles govern the poetic experience.

(In Defense of Reason)

Perhaps the most striking feature of this selection of the poems of Yvor Winters is the contrast in style and subject between the early poems, written before 1929, which are in experimental meters and forms, and the later poems, written in traditional English iambic meter and in a variety of traditional prosodic forms. Winters acknowledged this change in his poetic practice in the preface to *The Early Poems* (1966), explaining that it was not a "sudden intellectual or religious conversion." Rather he found that he could not write poems of the quality he admired in Baudelaire, Valéry, Hardy, Bridges, and Stevens—"in a few poems each"—by the method he was using, so he changed his method, "explored the new method," and later came to understand the "theoretical reasons for the change" he had made as a practical necessity (13).

His exploration of the reasons led him to write the critical essays and books enumerated above. His achievement made him the most innovative American literary critic of the period after 1930. Donald E. Stanford writes that Winters is "the only important poet of the century to go from experimental to traditional poetic technique" and "the only critic of the twentieth century who formulated a coherent theory of poetry at the same time he was practicing it" (*Revolution and Convention in Modern Poetry* [Newark: Univ. of Delaware Press, 1983], 191).

Winters is often called a New Critic, because his work was developed in dialogue with R. P. Blackmur, Kenneth Burke, John Crowe Ransom, Cleanth Brooks, Allen Tate, and others during the 1930s and 1940s, but he does not properly belong to that group. In effect, he retheoretized the function of the poem and of criticism in a way that they did not. He belongs, rather, in the line of major literary critics in English that runs from Sidney and Ben Jonson through Dryden, Samuel Johnson, Coleridge, and Matthew Arnold. There is more to be learned from his deeply thought-out resistance to the seductions and limitations of Modernity than from any other critic, because he attacked the relativistic principles that have led in recent years to the near destruction in the universities of both poetry and criticism itself.

For the most part Winters stood apart from the established norms and ideas of modern literature. Yet Kenneth Fields suggests in a memoir that "his approach is less marked by a distinct philosophy, method, or theory than we have sometimes supposed." He is not a theorist in the modern sense of "a theory," which Wesley Trimpi has described "as an idea to be tested, a body of doctrine to be believed, or a program to be instituted." Rather, Winters is a theorist in the older Greek sense of "viewing" or "observing" (*theoria*), in Trimpi's phrase: "inclusive observation or contemplation" (*Sequoia* [autumn 1984]: 60).

Because Winters's discussions of T. S. Eliot challenged the critical establishment and because generally his views on literature and on the most highly regarded poets of the time were assertively evaluative and written in a forthright and deliberate manner, he gained the reputation of being a "dogmatist" and a "formalist"—neither of which he was. As a practical critic, he may more aptly be called a connoisseur—a connoisseur who gives his reasons. Despite some negative reaction provoked by his views, the evaluations he made, in critical essays beginning in the 1920s, of such writers as Melville, Henry James, Edith Wharton, Emily Dickinson, and the experimentalists Wallace Stevens, Marianne Moore, William Carlos Williams, Hart Crane, Mina Loy, and others had a significant effect in winning a place in American studies for these authors.

Winters's idea of what poetry is and should be, at its best, can be touched on only briefly here. On the one hand, he opposed the idea of the poem as an autonomous aesthetic object—the art-for-the-sake-of-art school of criticism. On the other hand, he was never sympathetic to the didacticism of the socially conscious Marxist and socialist critics of the 1930s and 1940s, although he was always concerned for social justice. (One of the last poems he published in the *New Republic* is a sharp satirical comment on race relations in the South in 1957: "A White Spiritual," in *The Uncollected Poems of Yvor Winters 1929–1957*.) Although like the New Critics he is intensely interested in analysis of poetic technique, unlike them he places the function of poetry in a far broader context, that of the human consciousness as a whole. While analyzing the finest points of meter, rhythm, and the connotative associations of a word, he never loses sight of the essential function of the poem as a "technique of contemplation" and as a "moral evaluation"—two of his central repeated phrases. In defining poetry he places it beside other genres of writing such as philosophical meditation, as in Descartes, or the essay, as in Montaigne, though different in methods.

In the broad realm to which Winters assigns poetry, he gives it a high place, repeating at several times in his essays that the poetic discipline "is the richest and most perfect technique of contemplation." It is not a technique which would "eliminate the need of philosophy or of religion, but [one] which, rather, completes and enriches them" (*In Defense of Reason*, 21–22, 29). Moreover, Winters argues many times in his essays that the poem, more particularly, expresses and communicates a unique moral judgment of the experience contemplated.

Winters's assertions that poetry is a technique of contemplation and that poetry is a "moral evaluation"—or "moral judgment"—of experience have frequently been misunderstood. The word "moral" has unfortunately triggered visceral reactions in careless readers anxious to declare their freedom from any and all moral considerations in the realm of any art. What he means by "moral" as used in those two central phrases and in his essay title, "The Morality of Poetry," in *Primitivism and Decadence* (*In Defense of Reason*, 17), is not to say that the poet measures experience against some societal norm, or that poetry is essentially didactic, as was the belief and practice of most of the Marxist and socialist poets, nor that poetry should "teach a lesson" in the Victorian sense. For Winters "moral" means the properly or uniquely human function of the consciousness in establishing a balance within itself of conceptual thought and various emotive and other pressures. The *balance* of the consciousness is a key concept by which to grasp his self-understanding and his poetry and criticism. He thinks of Classical reason (the Platonic and Aristotelian *nous*) as the principle of order within the paradoxical human consciousness.

When Winters, Janet Lewis, and Howard Baker named the little literary magazine they started in 1929 the *Gyroscope,* they were thinking of the familiar scientific instrument, capable of maintaining its orientation and direction-keeping properties even in changing circumstances. It is used in spinning-tops and compasses and, today, in automatic pilots and ballistic missiles. The founders of the magazine intended the gyroscope as a symbol for the balance of the human consciousness as ordered by reason—Classical *nous,* not Enlightenment rationalism.

Such a Classical conception of reason, though not fully articulated in his critical writings, became central to Winters's understanding of the complex and paradoxical nature of the human consciousness. It is both Platonic and Aristotelian to think of the consciousness as structured by what Plato calls the "metaxy," or in-between condition, as the political philosopher Eric Voegelin has described the nature of the soul for both philosophers. Whether Winters derived this understanding of the consciousness from reading the Greek philosophers or from some later transmission, or simply from his own experience, it distinguishes him from most other modern critics.

For Winters, in art as in life, "moral judgment," as he uses the term, is a matter of comprehensive balance of the powers of the soul and the pressures on it in its in-between state, not of disregard for any aspect of the consciousness, much less of suppression, were such suppression possible. It was a chronic imbalance in the expression of the claims of emotion in the work of most nineteenth-century poets that led Winters to devalue their work. The most fully human, most fully conscious poet, in a quest for understanding, would appeal not only to similar experience of balance in his reader but to a similar capacity for rational thought and judgment about the experience that is the subject of the poem. Grosvenor Powell writes that most of Winters's negative critics "make the mistake of assuming that moral judgment is a wholly unlived and objective act," rather than, as it was for Winters, "always a lived experience": "It is only moral because it is human; there is always an element of feeling, and . . . the moral judgment is expressed through the human feeling motivated by the poem" (Introduction, *Yvor Winters: An Annotated Bibliography, 1919–1982* [Metuchen, N.J.: Scarecrow Press, 1983], 11).

Throughout his critical work Winters remained close to the fundamental questions that must be asked about poetry and about literature generally, if literature is to survive. His work shows no inclination to spin fine webs of "theory" in the spider-like manner that presently dominates the critical world of the academy and literary scholarship. Nor was he inclined to go extensively into biographical or historical influences and origins, though he always made use of the most authoritative historical scholarship that he could find in seeking understanding of a text or tracing the influence of ideas. His last published poem, included here, was dedicated to his friend in the English department at Stanford, the esteemed Old English philologist, Herbert Dean Meritt, of whom he wrote: "With cool persistent tact, / You form what men would say." Another esteemed Old English philologist, Fred Robinson, observes in a review of *Forms of Discovery* Winters's "imaginative understanding of the exact point where philological scholarship, literary criticism and the writing of poetry . . . share a common concern and exact an equal measure of seriousness from their practitioners" (*Comparative Literature Studies* 5 [1968]: 489).

His criticism nearly always focuses on a particular work, on what it was meant to say, as far as that can be understood, and on how the writer put it together technically. The critic's final and most important task, after understanding the work on its own terms and in its context, is, for Winters, to evaluate it generally and in relationship to others of its kind, giving reasons for his evaluation, whether positive or negative. In *The Function of Criticism* he writes that "the primary function of criticism is evaluation, and that unless criticism succeeds in providing a usable system of evaluation it is worth very little" (16–17).

Useful in reading Winters's poems in this selection is an awareness of his view of how language is used in poems and how it can attain a maximum effect. He qualifies his central definition of poetry as "a statement in words about a human experience" by writing that it is a statement "in which special pains are taken with the expression of feeling" ("Preliminary Problems," *In Defense of Reason*, 363). Words are "audible sounds," or their "visual symbols." Simple enough. But next he makes a distinction between the conceptual meaning of a word and its connotations, a thick penumbra of historical and personal associations that meaning carries with it. Both conceptual and perceptual content are extremely important in Winters's criticism, but understanding of the conceptual meaning should precede response to the emotion elicited.

There are a number of reasons for this. First, most of the emotional impact of a poem is, or should be, derivative from the conceptual content itself—from what the poem actually says. Second, what he calls "the vague associations of feeling" that cling around nearly all words can and should relate coherently, justly, and precisely to what is said conceptually. The feelings and emotional associations evoked by the words should stand in a rational, comprehensible, and just relationship to the statement (the motive).

Winters composed his critical books, essays, and reviews the way he composed most of his poems: so that every word counts. There is little filler. He says what he has to say as clearly and compactly as he can, not troubling to refute objections he feels he has answered elsewhere. Such plainness brings the reader into touch with the essential and perennial questions.

Yet his style brought him some misunderstanding. John Fraser writes in a review of *Forms of Discovery* that in his earlier books "too much of the essential evidence [for his evaluations] was produced only dispersedly." However, in his last book, as in the "final stages of a painting . . . the whole canvas is retouched and the relations of all the parts to each other are fully clarified at last" (*Southern Review* 5 [1969]: 185). Winters completes the argument made throughout his essays by a full chronological discussion and by listing over four hundred poems for commendation: "Almost every kind of short poem is among them, almost every kind of subject, and almost every kind of form and technique." Further, after noting some of the faults of the book which are for him "venial," Fraser writes that what "distinguishes Winters among poetic historians is not only his unwavering concern with the particularity of the poems and poets he discusses and with their relative merits," but also "his concern with the dynamics of poetic history in terms of first-rate states of consciousness." By this he draws attention to Winters's discrimination of a canon of poems in the English language that includes the work of poets so various as Raleigh, Jonson, Vaughan,

Churchill, Dickinson, Hardy, Stevens, and Bogan. Whether the effect of Winters's criticism is permanent remains to be seen. I would hazard the view that unless it is, the role of poetry in the intellectual and cultural life of the mind in the twenty-first century will have lost its most serious and passionate defender.

Discoveries: The Experimental Poems of the 1920s

In this the sound of wind is like a flame.

("The Rows of Cold Trees")

Some slight commentary—by no means full explications—may be helpful to the reader who is encountering Winters's poetry for the first time here. The first three poems in R. L. Barth's selection are the first poems that the poet chose to reprint in *The Early Poems of Yvor Winters 1919–1928* (1966). "Two Songs of Advent" and "One Ran Before" appeared in *The Immobile Wind*, published when he was twenty-one. The next five one-line poems appeared in *The Magpie's Shadow*, a book of twenty-eight poems composed entirely in this unusual six-syllable trimeter form, not really free verse. Appearing in the first "Song" and throughout many of the early poems is the theme of the human consciousness alone in the physical universe, expressed in terms of austere western American landscapes. The landscapes are those of New Mexico, Colorado, and Idaho, all places he lived while recovering from tuberculosis. The solitary consciousness is represented as a voice in relationship to a landscape.

In the first "Song," the landscape is an "ancient shell," hostile, enormous (voices are only "far whispers"), alien, and isolating to the human being's unique but fragile trait of articulate thought. In the second "Song," the "coyote" has a voice, "running wild in the wind's valleys," but he is regarded as hostile, for he proposes to take over the consciousness: "I enter now your thought." In this and in other early poems Winters uses the Native American poetic form of speaking in the persona of an animal or some other less-than-human condition, as a technique to explore the imagined experience of the non-human—a dissolution of the consciousness. For examples: "Alone" (a dissolution), "Winter Echo," and "The Aspen's Song."

Nearly all writers on the early poems have noticed the importance of contemporary Imagist experimental poetry, of Japanese poetry, and of Native American poetry to Winters's sensibility and technique. Terry Comito, in discussing the unique quality of Native American poetry, comments in *In Defense of Winters: The Poetry and Prose of Yvor Winters* (Madison: Univ. of Wisconsin Press, 1986), "It would scarcely be an exaggeration to say that the use of language in *The Magpie's Shadow* is a magical one: the book is a series of charms to summon up beneficent powers and to banish malignant ones" (55). Again, after carefully analyzing these influences and Winters's success with them, the British poet Dick Davis notes in *Wisdom and Wilderness: The Achievement of Yvor Winters* (Athens: Univ. of Georgia Press, 1983), that Winters is "attempting to convey sensation through language, and language, his means of communication, seems to get in the way":

> His later insistence on words as *concepts*, mental signs separate from the world, is a direct result of his early attempt to "give" sensation unmediated to the reader. He came to believe that language was irreducibly a matter of the intellect and could not convey pure sensation —the attempt was the pursuit of an ignis fatuus (14).

One may add that in his pursuit, especially in the one-liners of *The Magpie's Shadow*, he produced some of the most beautiful poems of the Imagist movement. Again, noticing the limitations of the sensibility and technique in these poems, Kenneth Fields comments in "Forms of the Mind: The Experimental Poems of Yvor Winters" (*Southern Review* 17 [1981]) that "in Winters's early poems reality seems to be a solipsistic function of the poet's mind, an invention, not a discovery" (941). Yet "discovery of reality" was what Winters later came to believe poetry was all about.

Grosvenor Powell provides a fascinating analysis of Winters's handling of the subject-object problem, as a prime concern of his early intellectual dilemma, inherited from Romanticism:

> The relationship between subject and object in experience is often discussed as if it were a polarity: perceiver and perceived, self and nonself, internal and external. It is only a polarity, however, when considered schematically and statically. In experience, the two poles

fuse inextricably—the intensity of the experience determining the degree of fusion. In the most intense moments of vision, the polarity disappears.

The fusion entails loss of consciousness—that is, oblivion. And Winters saw oblivion as death, and rejected it (*Language as Being in the Poetry of Yvor Winters* [Baton Rouge: Louisiana State Univ. Press, 1980], 126–27). The poet himself, of course, saw all these limitations, though not always in these terms, criticized them in his essays, and turned to write another kind of poetry in about 1929.

Winters appears in retrospect not to have lost much through his early experimental poetry, though he personally regretted the years he lingered under the spell of the ignis fatuus of poetic "immediacy." Rather, one positive result clearly was a carryover of a lifelong solicitude for exact sensory detail in any phrase or descriptive line within a poem written in traditional meter and form. Fields notes that despite changing his "methods and ideas in later years, he preserves much of his early imagist subtlety" (952), as, for example, in the line describing the ocean in "The Slow Pacific Swell" (1931): "Heaving and wrinkled in the moon and blind." With its fusion of two perceptions, of the sea surface seen sharply as itself and suggesting simultaneously its powerful inhabitant the gray whale, Winters's apprenticeship to imagist technique shows its value. "Summer Commentary," one of Winters's finest later poems, likewise achieves stunning effects of sensory sharpness, perceptual exactness, and juxtaposition of perceptions.

Transitional Investigations

No man can hold existence in the head.

("The Moralists")

Howard Baker, Winters's early friend and fellow poet, writes in his retrospective essay, "'The Gyroscope'" (*Southern Review* 17 [1981]), that 1929 "was the year of the foundation of his later work" (735). Winters believed that the *Gyroscope* stood for "an approximation of a classical state of mind"—an approximation which could only be developed, as Winters wrote in his statement of editorial purpose, by the "study of the masters of art and thought, as well as of self and living human relations" (735, 738). In this compact statement, Winters identified a program for his own intellectual and poetic development. His poems written over the next thirty years show to which "masters of art and thought" he turned and from whom he learned, as well as the fruits of his study of himself and his "living human relations."

For example, his study of one master of thought led to his treatment of the life and intentions of Socrates, in the moving internal monologue "Socrates," and, together with another historical figure, to a significant stanza in a poem not included here, "A Testament (to One Now a Child)": "These gave us life through death: / Jesus of Nazareth, archaic Socrates." The double heritage of American civilization in the Judaeo-Christian and the Graeco-Roman body of art and thought is compactly alluded to in two central historical figures, as part of a deeply personal reflection upon a parent-child relationship: "O small and fair of face, / In this appalling place / The conscious soul must give / Its life to live"—the tragic concept exemplified in the lives of both historical figures mentioned. Other masters of art and thought appear in many different poems.

Yet, obviously, so major a turn-around in style and life could not be instantly accomplished. In a sense, Winters remained "experimental" through a transitional period from 1928 to 1931 during which he was editing the *Gyroscope* and contributing as Western editor of *Hound & Horn*. After first applying his acute intelligence and talent to experiments in modern verse, he turned, in effect, to experiments in traditional meters and forms, for even in the latter he created something entirely new. He found that more could be done—could be said about contemporary experience—in poems that engaged *all* of the consciousness than in those that engaged only the sensibility. The "extension and reintegration of the spirit," as he termed his endeavor, could be best achieved by using all the resources of the mind and senses that language afforded. But first some problems had to be cleared up, even if they stretched the resources of at least one traditional form to the breaking point.

His first exercises in traditional form were sonnets that appeared in the *Gyroscope* and in *American Caravan* (collected in *The Proof*), of which six are included here. They are, as Douglas Peterson suggests, a sequential exploration by the poet of the role of the mind "in working out of solipsism," out of "the prison of his own subjectivity" (*Southern Review* 17 [1981]: 919). They show Winters experimenting with direct expression about an epistemological question: How does the mind deal with immediacy, in particular with the brutal fact of death, whether that of others or its own mortality? Such a question had to be dealt with satisfactorily before he could emerge from the solipsistic concerns of the early poems to a balanced consciousness founded on rationality as the ordering principle. As Richard Hoffpauir writes in a recent essay, "Strategies of Knowing: The *Proof* Sonnets of Yvor Winters,"

> It is entirely appropriate that he chose this form to investigate the conventional ways of placing and moving the significance-seeking mind between unstable and finally unknowable mutability of the physical on the one hand and the unstable and finally unknowable immutability of the absolute on the other hand. (*English Studies in Canada* 23 [1997]: 75)

Two of the poles of the consciousness in its in-between condition, time and the timeless, were obsessive concerns of Winters in his earlier poems. Hoffpauir writes that in "To William Dinsmore Briggs Conducting His Seminar" Winters found that "The definable is never completely free of the indefinable; we can never break free into pure truth; the absolute can never be viewed separate from the impure." Nor, it may be added, can the timeless ever be viewed, by us, separate from time. The poet, as student, "detects the effort, the successes, and the limitations in the very face of his teacher Briggs (lines 11–13)."

Discoveries: The Later Poems in Traditional Meters and Forms

> All this to pass, not to return again.
>
> ("The Marriage")

Study of the "self," announced in the *Gyroscope* manifesto, from this point on always led Winters *outward* from the closed consciousness that had been the preoccupation of his early poems—and of modernity generally—into "living human relations": family, friends, fellow poets and critics, academic colleagues, and contemporary American public life, whether local or national. Thus, the later poems directly concern, first, such subjects as love and marriage, children, parents, and friends. Second, they concern public figures, historical and contemporary, and public events. Third, many concern the life of the mind as evident in both art and scholarship. And last, he wrote several poems on the human relationship to the Divine, or as he variously termed it, the "Eternal Spirit," the "Holy Spirit," or the "Absolute."

Having explored a major epistemological concern in the sonnet form in a style aptly characterized by Hoffpauir as marked by a "too urgent bluntness," Winters turned to the possibilities of the traditional heroic couplet, with its two iambic pentameter rhymed lines. Almost immediately, he found it a more congenial form than the sonnet. He wrote a magnificent group of six poems, "The Slow Pacific Swell," "The Marriage," "On a View of Pasadena from the Hills," "The Journey," "A Vision," and "The Grave" (not included here), all collected in 1931 in *The Proof*. Each one deals with personal experience, and yet through the "innovation" in style, the return to expository statement and traditional meter, each relates the personal to common experience in lucid but deeply felt language.

When he writes in "A View of Pasadena" that "This is my father's house," the conceptual language draws the reader into reflection upon his own child-parent relationship. The relationship of American urban civilization to the land, a major theme in American thought, is also richly explored in Winters's meditation on the Los Angeles suburbs (discussed further below). More than any other poem of this period of his writing, "A View of Pasadena" illustrates what Winters meant when he wrote in his introduction to *Early Poems* (1966) that he found he could not achieve in experimental verse what he could in traditional meters.

Although in his *Gyroscope* manifesto Winters set out a program for study of the masters of art and thought and of living human relationships, he failed to mention that the relationship between man and the physical universe of which he is a part would be an abiding theme for him. A preoccupation with the human consciousness existing in a hostile universe is present in his poetry from beginning to end in many experiential differentiations. Even in one of the last poems he wrote, "To the Holy Spirit (from a Deserted Graveyard in the Salinas Valley"), the natural world is still felt, as it was in most of the early poems, in subtly hostile terms. He describes the landscape setting in the Salinas Valley (California) as "desert," "pure line" (like the "pale mountains" of "Advent I"), "dry grass and sand," that offers "no vision to distract"—that is, nothing beyond its blunt inarticulate presence. Yet the hills' appearance is deceptive, for "Calm in deceit, they stay."

Despite a lingering preoccupation with an intuited malignity in nature, throughout the poems in traditional meters and forms from 1930 on (especially in the series written in heroic couplets) Winters explores some of the more benign or at least more secure relationships that man can establish with different kinds of landscapes through growth in emotional and intellectual maturity and through civilized efforts. For Winters these are achieved through reason, exercise of will, and deliberated action. Still, it must be kept in mind, as the Canadian critic John Baxter cautions in "Can Winters Mean What He Says?" that the kind of "definitive certainty that Winters frequently manages to convey in his tone should not be allowed to obscure the profoundly exploratory quality of many of his poems, almost all of which have an unmistakably American timbre" (*Southern Review* 17 [1981]: 842–43).

A few examples will suffice. In "The Slow Pacific Swell," although the Pacific Ocean is felt to be at least as threatening to human life and consciousness as the arid stony Western deserts and mountains of the early poems, yet the poet is able to stand apart ("A landsman I, the sea is but a sound") in a balanced poise appropriate to his humanity. Moreover, he is acutely aware of the sensory beauties of the land: "The rain has washed the dust from April day." In "The Marriage," nature is seen in his garden in its most lovely and delicate sensory details: "The lacy fronds of carrots in the spring, / Their flesh sweet on the tongue," and "The young kids bleating softly in the rain."

In the uniquely powerful poem, "On a View of Pasadena from the Hills," Winters develops in a very different way his theme of hostile nature. Nature, as "cold and monstrous stone," underlies and yet is challenged by the developing civilization of Los Angeles and its suburbs in the late 1920s. Detail by detail, as he watches the day begin from his father's house in Eagle Rock (Flintridge), overlooking "the city, on the tremendous valley floor," the poet elucidates what the scene means to him and the costs of such a civilization. For example: "The driver, melting down the distance here, / May cast in flight the faint hoof of a deer / Or pass the faint head set perplexedly." The poem is comprehensive in its description and not limited to ephemeral appearances of Los Angeles at the time. It offers historical detail (in his childhood "The palms were coarse; their leaves hung thick with dust"); personal detail (of his father: "Too firmly gentle to displace the great"); and immediate visual detail ("The long leaves of the eucalypti screen / The closer hills from view—lithe, tall, and fine, / And nobly clad with youth, they bend and shine"). The reader may easily track the variations on the theme of nature partially subdued by human effort and the kind of precarious balance achieved in this poem, as in "The Slow Pacific Swell."

Nature is again perceived as dangerous in a later poem, "Elegy on a Young Airedale Bitch Lost Some Years Since in the Salt-Marsh" (*Before Disaster*, 1934), but here the setting is the relatively benign salt marshes of the southern edge of San Francisco Bay. The canine victim is "betrayed by what is wild" in her. Another small poem that shows a similar preoccupation with the constant material (and sometimes spiritual) presence of "the brutal earth we feared" is "Much in Little" (1938), where he writes about a corner of his garden: "And if no water touch the dust / In some far corner, and one dare / To

xxxv

breathe upon it, one may trust / The spectre on the summer air: / The risen dust alive with fire, / The fire made visible." This particular preoccupation and Winters's insistence upon achieving a balance of consciousness and maintaining it through deliberate effort of the will and intelligence is, perhaps, best summed up in the line in "To a Portrait of Herman Melville in My Library" (not included here) praising Melville's literary and personal achievement: "Wisdom and wilderness are here at poise."

Other less directly personal poems that develop the theme of nature and civilization include the dramatic monologue "John Sutter" (1935), in which Winters splendidly evokes the pre–Gold Rush Central Valley landscape in all its pastoral beauty. He suggests that a civilized man, when he cultivates the land and does not exploit it for greed, can make the natural seem benign. John Sutter, the Swiss immigrant, describes his ranch and farm lands: "The earth grew dense with grain at my desire; / The shade was deepened at the spring and streams," and he aids the settlers, who "in my houses feasted through the nights, / Rebuilt their sinews and assumed a name." Yet when gold is discovered, the settlers, "grained by alchemic change," become themselves mindless, like the rock and minerals: "Metal, intrinsic value, deep and dense, / Preanimate, inimitable, still, / Real, but an evil with no human sense, / Dispersed the mind to concentrate the will."

Yet another differentiation of the theme of nature in relationship to man emerges when the roles become reversed and man's civilizing activity reveals an intention to overcome nature rather than to live in harmony with it. In "The California Oaks" (1936), Winters reviews the history of the majestic native oaks, first through the Native American generations: "What feet have come to roam, / what eyes to stay?" A conjectural Chinese period follows: "Hwui-Shan, the ancient, for a moment glides [and] The brook-like shadows lie / where sun had shone." Next, the English, "Drake and his seamen pause to view the hills," and the Spaniard, because he learned "caution from the trees," allows his "ambitious mind" to bend "to an archaic way." None of these harmed the oaks. However, with "the invasion" of the American settlers, "the soil was turned, / The hidden waters drained, the valley dried" and the oaks begin to die out.

In an anticipation of our turn-of-millennium concern with the increasing pace of destruction of plant and other kinds of life, the poet eulogizes "the archaic race— / Black oak, live oak, and valley oak," who have "Died or are dying!"

Winters carries this reversal in the roles of nature and man to an extreme variation and defines the dangers of man to nature and consequently, of course, to himself because he is part of nature, in his poem, "An Elegy: For the U.S.N. Dirigible, Macon" (1938). The poem is about the construction, launching, and loss in a storm in February, 1935, of the lighter-than-air craft, which was 785 feet long. The airship was launched from Moffett Field in Sunnyvale, not far from the home of the poet and his wife on the outskirts of Palo Alto. As Steven Shankman has pointed out, the dirigible becomes a symbol of mankind's hubristic desire to achieve perfection in building a "flawless technological machine," one that will rival nature in power: "The perfect wheel / Now glides on perfect surface with a sound / Earth has not heard before" (*In Search of the Classic: Reconsidering the Greco-Roman Tradition* [University Park: Pennsylvania State Univ. Press, 1994], 36–48).

As Shankman reads it, the poem is a strong critique of "rationalism," in distinction from "rationality," the term by which he distinguishes the balance of consciousness based on Classical reason. He compares Winters's judgment of the *Macon's* builders to that of Sophocles in his indictment of Athenian pride of intellect in *Oedipus Tyrannos*. Oedipus is a "symbol of the . . . desire to master reality, to know it from the outside rather than patiently to participate in it; he is a symbol, that is, of rationalism rather than of rationality." Winters is saying that "in place of a profound awareness of the need for spiritual salvation, modern man has substituted the rationalist dream of mastering the material world, an enterprise which can only lead to suicide both spiritual and material" (46–47). Man trying to overcome nature will destroy his hard-won civilization: the present age has "seized upon a planet's heritage / Of steel and oil, the mind's viaticum: / Crowded the world with strong ingenious things, / Used the provision it could not replace; / To leave but Cretan myths." In this poem and in others, whether they deal with excesses of "rationalism," on the one hand, or excesses of feeling, on the other,

Winters always views the problem from the balanced center of the consciousness—the centered poise of Classical reason as he understood it from 1929 on.

Such a balance is reflected, again in terms of civilized and social culture, in "Time and the Garden" (*Poems*, 1940), where the poet's pleasure in his own garden of "Persimmon, walnut, loquat, fig, and grape" symbolizes the integration of the sensory and intellectual aspects of the consciousness that he has, momentarily at least, achieved. The change of seasons is experienced in a way quite unlike the stark obsessive impressions of the early sequences in *The Bare Hills*. They are spaced by the cultivated plants "in their due series" and make his garden "a tranquil dwelling place." Yet even here, as a man, Winters knows himself to be capable of imbalance, and he recognizes his own peculiar temptation to impatience, "restlessness," in his quest for "Unbroken wisdom" and for the achievement of the poets whom he admires, "Gascoigne, Ben Jonson, Greville, Raleigh, Donne" (all of whom he discusses in detail in his critical essays).

Last, in both style and subject, "A Summer Commentary" (1938) is the finest example of Winters's continuity with his early poems, even while the result of his commitment to the classical balance of the consciousness is evident. In plain language he recalls in the first stanza his early state of mind, when "with sharper sense," hearing "the farthest insect cry," he was "stayed" by it, while, "intense," he "watched the hunter and the bird." Then, in precise conceptual language, he questions that earlier experience. What meaning did he find then, or was it "but a state of mind, / Some old penumbra of the ground, / In which to be but not to find?" The word "penumbra" alone, with its connotations of overarching, heavy shadow, evokes the entire ambiance and feeling of the closed solipsistic consciousness of the early poems. The wordless immediacy of purely sensory "being" is contrasted with the truly human activity of seeking (questing) and finding more and more of reality. Then through the last three stanzas Winters describes his present feelings about the excessively dry, dusty, late summer California landscape in terms of the "sweet," the "fair," the "soft," and the "rich," in vivid visual, aural, tactile, and olfactory imagery, almost as if astonished by the pleasure and beauty revealed to him in this landscape.

The perceptions are conveyed with the sharp impact of the imagist technique, while the intimate directness and firm conceptual statement of the opening two stanzas control and give meaning to the sensory passages. Now, "summer grasses, brown with heat, / Have crowded sweetness through the air; / The very roadside dust is sweet; / Even the unshadowed earth is fair." And "silence," which had in the early poems been the "silence" of mindless absorption in "stone," "lichen," "leaves," or "bees," is now "caressed" by the "soft voice of the nesting dove, / And the dove in soft erratic flight." Even the "rubble, the fallen fruit," though doomed to "decay," as is everything in nature, produces by its fermenting the sweetness of "brandy."

Winters's poems that take man in nature as their subject represent only one of the many kinds of poetry he wrote. As part of his announced intention to move out into living human relations, he published throughout his career a number of poems on public and historical figures, and on public events, as well as poems on the purpose and hazards of art and the artist in society. On public figures or on the role of the political man, in this collection, are the Machiavellian "The Prince," the worldly American "On the Death of Senator Thomas J. Walsh," and his allegorical narrative of a man of action, "Theseus: A Trilogy." On historical figures are "Socrates," "John Day, Frontiersman," "John Sutter," and "On Rereading a Passage from John Muir." On his participation in public experience are two of the Depression era: "Before Disaster" (when "Fool and scoundrel guide the state") and "By the Road to the Air-Base." The following concern World War II: "Summer Noon 1941," "To a Military Rifle" (probably the finest, with its indictment of the lust for power), "Moonlight Alert," "Defense of Empire," "Night of Battle" (for the last two see *The Collected Poems of Yvor Winters*, ed. Donald Davie, 1978), and "Epitaph for the American Dead" (for this see *The Uncollected Poems of Yvor Winters 1929–1957*, ed. R. L. Barth, 1997). He wrote several poems on the trial and defense of David Lamson in San Jose (1933–37), a series of events in which Winters engaged both his sympathy and his efforts for Lamson's acquittal (for these also see *Collected Poems*, 1978).

As a result of his study of the "masters of art," as well as the "masters of thought," Winters frequently writes of both the artist and the scholar in terms of the life of the mind. Some of these poems are general in theme, some personal, and some achieve both the general and personal by using a Greek mythical figure or a medieval legend. Among the more general are "To a Young Writer," "Sonnet to the Moon," and "On Teaching the Young." More personal is a long and gently funny satire in heroic couplets on many of the celebrated poets and critics of the 1920s: "The Critiad: A Poetical Survey of Recent Criticism" (1931). It is imitative of Pope, but without Pope's acid tone (see *The Uncollected Poems 1929–1957*). More personal in subject are "For Howard Baker" and poems addressed to Emily Dickinson, Herman Melville, and Nathaniel Hawthorne (not included here).

Under the Greek figure of "Orpheus," Winters writes of his early friend and fellow poet Hart Crane. In "Heracles," he writes, as he noted, "of the artist in hand-to-hand or semi-intuitive combat with experience." In this poem, which has been misinterpreted, the artist, in the figure of the Greek hero Heracles, loses his humanity because he loses the balance of the consciousness. In his attempt to achieve the "Absolute," he enters the "Timeless," as a demigod, but because he becomes "perfection," he sacrifices the imperfect woman Deïanira: "This was my grief, that out of grief I grew." Tragically, he grows beyond the human. In "Sir Gawaine and the Green Knight," based on a medieval legend, Winters writes of his own early experience of the attempt to achieve an immediacy with nature. In "Chiron," through the Greek mythical figure of the centaur who was Achilles' tutor, he writes of his attempts to educate young poets. In "Time and the Garden," he writes of his restlessness in striving to reach the achievements of the poets whom he admired. In one of the last poems he wrote, "To the Moon" (1953), the general and personal come together effortlessly, as he invokes the Moon, as the "Goddess of poetry," and writes that "Your service I have found / To be no sinecure; / For I must still inure / My words to what I find, / Though it should leave me blind / Ere I discover how" (*Collected Poems*, 1952, 1978).

As part of his commitment to the life of the mind, including the studies appropriate to a university scholar, Winters wrote several poems praising men engaged in scholarship. There are three on his graduate teacher at Stanford, the distinguished scholar of Renaissance humanism, William Dinsmore Briggs. Of these, included here are "To William Dinsmore Briggs Conducting His Seminar," "Dedication for a Book of Criticism," and "For the Opening of the William Dinsmore Briggs Room." Connected in theme is his one poem on a work of art, "On a Portrait of a Scholar of the Italian Renaissance." Of this type is "To Herbert Dean Meritt," mentioned above. Four poems, none included here, satirize academics who failed to live up to the profession. As early as 1946 Winters had analyzed the roots of the decay of American academic life in his essay "The Significance of *The Bridge* by Hart Crane, Or What Are We to Think of Professor X?" (*In Defense of Reason*, 577–603). Relativism and indifference in the pursuit of truth in the humanities, far beyond that of his "genteel" Professor X, had by the time of his death corrupted the life of the mind in the university and consequently the life of the art of poetry there.

In abandoning the self-engrossment typical of his (and other poets') work during the 1920s, Winters explored, perhaps more movingly than any other area of life, the relationships of love, marriage, children, and parents, frequently in the context of mortality. Of these the reader may turn to "The Dedication" (from *Before Disaster*), "Inscription for a Graveyard," "The Last Visit" (with its haunting line, "Ruin has touched familiar air"), and, as an especially illustrative example, "The Marriage." In an acute analysis of this poem as Winters's exploration of the "old question, what *is* love?" Gordon Harvey notes that the lovers "neither live wholly in each other (as would Tristan and Iseult in their vault, and sometimes Donne), nor try to fix their love in some perfect moment (like Jay Gatsby, and sometimes Donne)." Rather, "they look outward, and forward, in the same direction. After demonstrating Winters's use of metaphysical thought, Harvey concludes,

"The Marriage" in Winters's title is double, and in this his poem answers Donne. The marriage is first the indissoluble union of each of our spirits to its ever-changing phenomenal circumstances, including the body. This is the union [James] Smith shows to be such a positive wonder to Donne, and it is a ground theme in Winters's work as a whole, poetry *and* criticism. But the marriage is also what this first union seems to make unimaginable for Donne, and often enough for ourselves: a union of two spirits actually forged and deepened by separate selfhood, by change, and by the absoluteness of death. This is the metaphysical puzzle at the heart of civil marriage, to which enterprise Winters's poem attaches us. ("Winters's 'Marriage' and Donne," *The Gadfly: A Quarterly Review of English Letters* [May 1984]: 40–41)

Others of this type are "For My Father's Grave," "Phasellus Ille," "A Leave-Taking," "The Cremation," "Prayer for My Son," and one of his last poems, the exemplar of Winters's high art, "At the San Francisco Airport," addressed to his daughter. Others not included here on similar themes are "To My Infant Daughter" and "A Testament (to One Now a Child)," mentioned above (see *Collected Poems*, 1952, 1978).

Finally, in the widest casting of all in his quest for reality, Winters wrote several poems of a type his early manifesto did not apparently include in its program—those on the human relationship to God, or the Divine, or (the terms he uses) the Holy Spirit, the Eternal Spirit, or the Absolute. In "Prayer for My Son," he addresses the "Eternal Spirit" as "you / Whose will maintains the world, / Who thought and made it true;" and as "You who guided Socrates." In "To the Holy Spirit," he defines the Spirit as "mind alone" but also speaks of the Holy Spirit's "fallen sons." In "A Fragment" he rejects the Christian faith directly ("I cannot find my way to Nazareth"), and he goes on to say, "Thy will is death, / And this unholy quiet is thy peace. / Thy will be done; and let discussion cease." In "A Song in Passing," he concludes: "There is no other place. / The only thing I fear / Is the Almighty Face." God may be addressed, may be prayed to, has sons, may be feared, may to a certain extent be defined but cannot be understood, certainly not from within the paradox of the human consciousness.

In "To the Holy Spirit" Winters shows his maturest skills. These include mastery of the short trimeter line structured in irregularly rhymed stanzas of irregular lengths. Although he was fond enough of trimeter to use it in many poems, he more often used it in quatrains than in an irregular stanza, as he does in this poem. Its stylistic predecessors include "Prayer for My Son," "Summer Noon," "To a Military Rifle," and a few others. "To the Holy Spirit" shows what he was aiming for all the time in its perfection of rhythm, as the sentences, clauses, and phrases run over from line to line, pacing his thought to the stanzaic limits, yet allowing variation in stanza lengths to reinforce the closures of the thought. All this gives an air of unstudied elegance of form.

The movement of the line also exploits an ever-varying position for the caesura, when there is one, within the line. Winters may have learned this from Ben Jonson, writing in the Classical plain style. But he had, probably before ever reading Jonson carefully, composed an entire book in the iambic trimeter line, standing on its own as an individual poem: *The Magpie's Shadow*. So, it is more likely that from an early period he was fond of exploring by ear the possibilities this line offers. Constant practice in writing a line with close attention to the effects of each syllable, when there are only six available, as well as of each pause, no doubt played its part in the mastery he exhibits in "To the Holy Spirit." Some of the lines could stand alone and, given appropriate titles, be successful imagist poems. For example: "The Bare Hills:" "Calm in deceit they stay."

In overall structure "To the Holy Spirit" demonstrates understanding of the tripartite meditative form typical of, and possibly learned from, the seventeenth-century devotional poetry of the Metaphysical poets. As practiced by Donne, Vaughan, and others, the first part (stanza 1) "sets the scene" or subject to be the focus of meditation, in this case the Salinas Valley landscape. The second part (stanza 2) constitutes the "meditation proper," in which the poet states his thoughts about the subject. In the third part (stanzas 3 and 4) the poet "turns" to address an individual in a "colloquy," in this case, with the Holy Spirit. The unique adaptability of this traditional form is evident in Winters's skilled handling of it. He had been concerned all his life with the Western, later California, landscape as a symbol of the material universe. Here he compactly represents it in a few telling words and phrases, infused with connotations of beauty, deceptive stability, and the menace of death. Also, his lifelong concern with palpable fact, especially that of death, obvious in the many poems that take death as their subject, permits his thought to move both by association and by logic into the meditation in the second stanza. Last, the peculiar power of the third part of the meditative form, the "turn" or "colloquy," demonstrates itself in Winters's sudden, almost abrupt, almost accusatory address: "These are Thy fallen sons, / Thou whom I try to reach. / Thou whom the quick eye shuns, / Thou dost elude my speech." Continuing the address to the Divine through the last two stanzas, Winters defines his understanding of the Holy Spirit as "mind alone," and of himself as "bound / Pure mind to flesh and bone, / And flesh and bone to ground." Desiring "certainty," he is only certain of the difference between himself (and man in general) and the Holy Spirit. The final observation is a reluctant admission of the impossibility for him because of age and · experience to pursue the question any further.

Yet, despite the putting aside at last of questions that he had been concerned with all his life, the tone of the poem, the power and resonance of the form and of the language, suffused with intelligence and personal engagement, is such that one feels Winters is leaving the question open for others to explore. He thought of poetic forms as various means to discovery, as the title of his last critical work indicates. This particular traditional meditative form enabled him to discover where he stood on the most important, to him, of all questions, but his personal stance is not offered as one for all readers. It is his considered understanding and judgment of the question at issue. By participating in his judgment, through reading and understanding it fully, the reader may be enabled to discover further areas within his or her consciousness that had not before been available.

David Yezzi, in a recent essay, "The Seriousness of Yvor Winters," has said of Winters's criticism of poetry that, "as both a description of its enduring ills and a prescription for regaining much that has been lost to the lyric tradition in English, Winters's bitter pill is our long-overlooked and strongest medicine" (New Criterion, July 1997, 28). Of Winters's poetry, Yezzi comments: "As with Rilke's archaic torso . . . when each of today's more fashionable, self-expressive and wildly emotive poets looks on Winters's work, there is but one heart-felt message: you must change your life" (33). That Winters himself in an act of profound and admirable resistance to the closed consciousness and the relativisms of modernity did change not only his style but his entire artistic and intellectual life is evident in the poems collected here.

Helen Pinkerton Trimpi

The Selected Poems of
YVOR WINTERS

Two Songs of Advent

I.

On the desert, between pale mountains, our cries—
Far whispers creeping through an ancient shell.

II.

Coyote, on delicate mocking feet,
Hovers down the canyon, among the mountains,
His voice running wild in the wind's valleys.

Listen! Listen! for I enter now your thought.

One Ran Before

I could tell
Of silence where
One ran before
Himself and fell
Into silence
Yet more fair.

And this were more
A thing unseen
Than falling screen
Could make of air.

Song for a Small Boy
Who Herds Goats

Sweeter than rough hair
On earth there is none,
Rough as the wind
And brown as the sun.

I toss high my short arms
Brown as the sun,
I creep on the mountains
And never am done.

Sharp-hoofed, hard-eyed,
Trample on the sun!—
Sharp ears, stiff as wind,
Point the way to run!

Who on the brown earth
Knows himself one?
Life is in lichens
That sleep as they run.

Alone

I, one who never speaks,
Listened days in summer trees,
Each day a rustling leaf.

Then, in time, my unbelief
Grew like my running—
My own eyes did not exist,
When I struck I never missed.

Noon, felt and far away—
My brain is a thousand bees.

Winter Echo

Thin air! My mind is gone.

Spring Rain

My doorframe smells of leaves.

The Aspen's Song

The summer holds me here.

God of Roads

I, peregrine of noon.

A Deer

The trees rose in the dawn.

The Precincts of February

Junipers,
Steely shadows,
Floating the jay.
A man,

Heavy and ironblack,
Alone in the sun,
Threading the grass.
The cold,

Coming again
As spring
Came up the valley,
But to stay

Rooted deep in the land.
The stone-pierced shadows
Trod by the bird
For day on day.

José's Country

A pale horse,
Mane of flowery dust,
Runs too far
For a sound
To cross the river.

Afternoon,
Swept by far hooves
That gleam
Like slow fruit
Falling
In the haze
Of pondered vision.

It is nothing.
Afternoon
Beyond a child's thought,
Where a falling stone
Would raise pale earth,
A fern ascending.

The Upper Meadows

The harvest falls
Throughout the valleys
With a sound
Of fire in leaves.

The harsh trees,
Heavy with light,
Beneath the flame, and aging,
Have risen high and higher.

Apricots,
The clustered
Fur of bees,
Above the gray rocks of the uplands.

The hunter deep in summer.
Grass laid low by what comes,
Feet or air—
But motion, aging.

Moonrise

The branches,
jointed, pointing
up and out, shine
out like brass.

Upon the heavy
lip of earth
the dog

        at
moments is
possessed and screams:

The rising moon draws
up his blood and hair.

The Cold

Frigidity the hesitant
uncurls its tentacles
into a furry sun.
The ice expands
into an insecurity
that should appal
yet I remain, a son
of stone and of a
commentary, I, an epitaph,
astray in this
oblivion, this
inert labyrinth
of sentences that
dare not end. It
is high noon and
all is the more quiet
where I trace
the courses of the Crab
and Scorpion, the Bull,
the Hunter, and the Bear—
with front of steel
they cut an aperture
so clear across the
cold that it cannot
be seen: there is no
smoky breath, no
breath at all.

Digue Dondaine, Digue Dondon

Sun on the sidewalk
for the corpse to
pass through like the
dark side of a leaf

in the immobile
suddenness of spring
he stood there
in the streetlight
casting a long shadow
on the glassed begonias
madness under
his streaked eyelids

miles away the
cold plow in veined earth

the wind fled hovering
like swarming bees
in highest night

the streets paved with
the moon smooth to
the heels

       and he whirled off in

Time

           and pale and small
children that run shrieking
through March doorways
burst like bubbles
on the cold twigs
block on block away

Nocturne

Moonlight on stubbleshining
hills
whirls down upon me finer than geometry
and at my very
eyes it blurs and softens like a dream

In leafblack houses
linen smooth with sleep
and folded by cold life itself for limbs so definite

their passion is
persistent like a pane of glass

about their feet the clustered
birds are sleeping
heavy with incessant life

The dogs swim close to earth

A kildee rises
dazed and rolled amid the sudden blur of sleep
above the dayglare of the fields
goes screaming
off toward darker hills.

"Quod Tegit Omnia"

Earth darkens and is beaded
with a sweat of bushes and
the bear comes forth;
the mind, stored with
magnificence, proceeds into
the mystery of Time, now
certain of its choice of
passion but uncertain of the
passion's end.

         When
Plato temporizes on the nature
of the plumage of the soul the
wind hums in the feathers as
across a cord impeccable in
tautness but of no mind:

                Time,
the sine-pondere, most
imperturbable of elements,
assumes its own proportions
silently, of its own properties—
an excellence at which one
sighs.

        Adventurer in
living fact, the poet
mounts into the spring,
upon his tongue the taste of
air becoming body: is
embedded in this crystalline
precipitate of Time.

Song

Where I walk out
to meet you on the
cloth of burning
fields

the goldfinches
leap up about my
feet like angry
dandelions

quiver like a
heartbeat in the
air and are
no more

April

The little goat
crops
new grass lying down
leaps up eight inches
into air and
lands on four feet.
Not a tremor—
solid in the
spring and serious
he walks away.

The Cold Room

The dream
stands
in the night
above unpainted
floor and chair.

The dog is
dead asleep
and
will not move
for god or fire.

And from the
ceiling
darkness bends
a heavy flame.

The Barnyard

The wind appears
and disappears
like breath on a mirror
and between the hills
is only cold
that lies
beneath the stones
and in the grass.
The sleeping dog
becomes a
knot of twinging turf.
It was the
spring that left
this rubbish
and these scavengers
for ice to kill—
this old man
wrinkled in
the fear of hell, the
child that staggers
straight into
the clotting cold
with short fierce cries.

The Rows of Cold Trees

To be my own Messiah to the
burning end. Can one endure the
acrid, steeping darkness of
the brain, which glitters and is
dissipated? Night, the night is
winter and a dull man bending,
muttering above a freezing pipe;
and I, bent heavily on books; the
mountain, iron in my sleep and
ringing; but the pipe has frozen, haired with
unseen veins, and cold is on the eyelids: who can
remedy this vision?

                            I have walked upon
the streets between the trees that
grew unleaved from asphalt in a night of
sweating winter in distracted silence.

                                   I have
walked among the tombs—the rushing of the air
in the rich pines above my head is that which
ceaseth not nor stirreth whence it is:
in this the sound of wind is like a flame.

It was the dumb decision of the
madness of my youth that left me with
this cold eye for the fact; that keeps me
quiet, walking toward a
stinging end: I am alone,
and, like the alligator cleaving timeless mud,
among the blessèd who have Latin names.

Prayer beside a Lamp

Vasti quoque rector Olympi . . .
Non agat hos currus.

I pace beside my books and hear the
wind stop short against the house like
a pneumatic gasp of death.
The mind that lives on
print becomes too savage: print that
stings and shivers in the cold when
shingles rise and fall. O God,
my house is built of bone that bends.

Beyond the roof
the sky turns with an endless roaring and bears all
the stars. What could you do?
Could you climb up against the whirling
poles alone? Grind through the ghastly
twist of the sphere? Could you maintain
a foothold on the rising earth for
night on night and walk the
creaking floor?

The steady courage
of the humming oil drives back the
darkness as I drive back sweating death;
from out a body stricken by this thought, I
watch the night grow turgid on the stair—
I, crumbling, in the crumbling brain of man.

Vacant Lot

Tough hair like dead
grass over new and
hooves quick and
impatient the he-goat
looks round him
over frozen mud

        but
finds no mate

        hardeyed
and savage he
turns back and nips
the bitter grass

The Deep: A Service for All the Dead

Old concentrate of thought, ironveined and slow,
that willed itself and labored out of earth,
man grinds his plow through corrugated rock
and draws a wake that lasts a thousand years:
it thins and gathers, creeps up to the spot
where the brain vanished.

                Vanished in concentration,
shrank till he could not stir—
a thought worn small with use, a formula,
a motion, then a stasis, and then nothing.
And in the bent heart of the seething rock
slow crystals shiver, the fine cry of Time.

Demigod

I stand here
raging
my brain beaten

white with thudding
blood o
anvil of the gods

my lips a blaze
of stone move
up and down with

heavy blasphemy
that batters
life upon your brains

I, set here
for all Time·
to mark this crossroads

for these blinding fools

Orange Tree

Hard, oily,
sinuous,
your trunk,

black serpent,
struggling
with your weight of gold—

great strength
massed
against Time,

in angry pride
you hold out
lacquered life

the classic leaf.

Song of the Trees

Belief is blind! Bees scream!
Gongs! Thronged with light!

                  And I take
into light, hold light,
in light I live, I,
pooled and broken here,
to watch, to wake above you.

                  Sun,
no seeming, but savage
simplicity, breaks running
for an aeon, stops, shuddering, here.

The Goatherds

The trees are
the rayed pillars
of the sun where
small boys gather
seashells in the desert;
goats move here and there;
the small boys
shriek amid white rocks,
run at the river;
and the sky has
risen in red dust
and stricken
villages with distance
till the brown feet quiver
on the rock like
fallen eyelids and the
goat's hoof, tiny,
jet, is like a twig about
to burst in flame.

               And then
the motion once again like
tiny blossoms
far away beside the river
and the cries of
small boys like the
cries of birds at dawn.

The Vigil

To grind out bread by facing God!
                The elbows, bone wedged
into wood with stubborn grief; the hard face
gripping the mad night in the vision's vise.

The floor burns underfoot, atomic
flickering to feigned rigidity: God's
fierce derision, and outside the oak
is living slowly but is strong; it grips
a moment to a thousand years; and it
will move across our gasping
bodies in the end.

                This is no
place to wait out Time. To see you
strikes my heart with terror,
speeding Time to violence and death.

The thought, the leap, is measured: madness
will return to sanity. The pendulum. Here.
              Trapped in Time.

Simplex Munditiis

The goat nips yellow blossoms
shaken loose from rain—
with neck extended
lifts a twitching flower
high into wet air. Hard
humility the lot of man
to crouch beside
this creature in the dusk
and hold the mind clear;
to turn the sod,
to face the sod beside his door,
to wound it as his own flesh.
In the spring the blossoms
drown the air with joy,
the heart with sorrow.
One must think of this
in quiet. One must
bow his head and take
with roughened hands
sweet milk at dusk,
the classic gift of earth.

Sonnet

This God-envenomed loneliness, the stain
Of Deity, is eating out specific
Souls from nothingness, and the horrific
Writhing of a moment is our gain.
The mind bends backward, labors up the grain
To find a milieu amid slow nocturnal
Nothingness. O waste! O the infernal
Massacre of moments in His Brain.

Dead, all eternity is swift as light,
An instant with no end; and all the dead,
All the last moments riveted supreme,
Arrested tier on tier of static flight,
Arrested scream on scream that yields no scream,
Crash soundless thunder solid to my head.

The Moralists

You would extend the mind beyond the act,
Furious, bending, suffering in thin
And unpoetic dicta; you have been
Forced by hypothesis to fiercer fact.
As metal singing hard, with firmness racked,
You formulate our passion; and behind
In some harsh moment nowise of the mind
Lie the old meanings your advance has packed.

No man can hold existence in the head.
I, too, have known the anguish of the right
Amid this net of mathematic dearth,
And the brain throbbing like a ship at night:
Have faced with old unmitigated dread
The hard familiar wrinkles of the earth.

The Realization

Death. Nothing is simpler. One is dead.
The set face now will fade out; the bare fact,
Related movement, regular, intact,
Is reabsorbed, the clay is on the bed.
The soul is mortal, nothing: the dim head
On the dim pillow, less. But thought clings flat
To this, since it can never follow that
Where no precision of the mind is bred.

Nothing to think of between you and All!
Screaming processionals of infinite
Logic are grinding down receding cold!
O fool! Madness again! Turn not, for it
Lurks in each paintless cranny, and you sprawl
Blurring a definition. Quick! you are old.

To William Dinsmore Briggs
Conducting His Seminar

Amid the walls' insensate white, some crime
Is redefined above the sunken mass
Of crumbled years; logic reclaims the crass,
Frees from historic dross the invidious mime.
Your fingers spin the pages into Time;
And in between, moments of darkness pass
Like undiscovered instants in the glass,
Amid the image, where the demons climb.

Climb and regard and mean, yet not emerge.
And in the godless thin electric glare
I watch your face spun momently along
Till the dark moments close and wrinkles verge
On the definitive and final stare:
And that hard book will now contain this wrong.

The Invaders

They have won out at last and laid us bare,
The demons of the meaning of the dead,
Stripped us with wheel and flame. Oh, where they tread,
Dissolves our heritage of earth and air!
Till as a locomotive plunges through
Distance that has no meaning and no bound
Thundering some interminable sound
To inward metal where its motion grew—

Grew and contracted down through infinite
And sub-atomic roar of Time on Time
Toward meaning that its changing cannot find;
So, stripped of color of an earth, and lit
With motion only of some inner rime,
The naked passion of the human mind.

The Castle of Thorns

Through autumn evening, water whirls thin blue,
From iron to iron pail—old, lined, and pure;
Beneath, the iron is indistinct, secure
In revery that cannot reach to you.
Water it was that always lay between
The mind of man and that harsh wall of thorn,
Of stone impenetrable, where the horn
Hung like the key to what it all might mean.

My goats step guardedly, with delicate
Hard flanks and forest hair, unchanged and firm,
A strong tradition that has not grown old.
Peace to the lips that bend in intricate
Old motions, that flinch not before their term!
Peace to the heart that can accept this cold!

Apollo and Daphne

Deep in the leafy fierceness of the wood,
Sunlight, the cellular and creeping pyre,
Increased more slowly than aetherial fire:
But it increased and touched her where she stood.
The god had seized her, but the powers of good
Struck deep into her veins; with rending flesh
She fled all ways into the grasses' mesh
And burned more quickly than the sunlight could.

And all her heart broke stiff in leafy flame
That neither rose nor fell, but stood aghast;
And she, rooted in Time's slow agony,
Stirred dully, hard-edged laurel, in the past;
And, like a cloud of silence or a name,
The god withdrew into Eternity.

The Empty Hills

Flintridge, Pasadena

The grandeur of deep afternoons,
The pomp of haze on marble hills,
Where every white-walled villa swoons
Through violence that heat fulfills,

Pass tirelessly and more alone
Than kings that time has laid aside.
Safe on their massive sea of stone
The empty tufted gardens ride.

Here is no music, where the air
Drives slowly through the airy leaves.
Meaning is aimless motion where
The sinking hummingbird conceives.

No book nor picture has inlaid
This life with darkened gold, but here
Men passionless and dumb invade
A quiet that entrances fear.

Moonrise

The slow moon draws
The shadows through the leaves.
    The change it weaves
Eludes design or pause.

    And here we wait
In moon a little space,
    And face to face
We know the hour grows late.

    We turn from sleep
And hold our breath a while,
    As mile on mile
The terror drifts more deep.

    So we must part
In ruin utterly—
    Reality
Invades the crumbling heart.

    We scarce shall weep
For what no change retrieves.
    The moon and leaves
Shift here and there toward sleep.

Inscription for a Graveyard

When men are laid away,
Revolving seasons bring
New love, corrupting clay
And hearts dissevering.

Hearts that were once so fast,
Sickened with living blood,
Will rot to change at last.
The dead have hardihood.

Death is Eternity,
And all who come there stay.
For choice, now certainty.
No moment breaks away.

Amid this wilderness,
Dazed in a swarm of hours,—
Birds tangled numberless!—
Archaic Summer towers.

The dead are left alone—
Theirs the intenser cost.
You followed to a stone,
And there the trail was lost.

The Last Visit

For Henry Ahnefeldt, 1862–1929

The drift of leaves grows deep, the grass
Is longer everywhere I pass.
And listen! where the wind is heard,
The surface of the garden's blurred—
It is the passing wilderness.
The garden will be something less
When others win it back from change.
We shall not know it then; a strange
Presence will be musing there.
Ruin has touched familiar air,
And we depart. Where you should be,
I sought a final memory.

For Howard Baker

Now autumn's end draws down
Hard twilight by the door;
The wash of rain will drown
Our evening words no more.

Words we have had in store.
But men must move apart
Though what has gone before
Have changed the living heart.

Music and strength of art
Beneath long winter rain
Have played the living part,
With the firm mind for gain.

Nor is the mind in vain.

The Slow Pacific Swell

Far out of sight forever stands the sea,
Bounding the land with pale tranquillity.
When a small child, I watched it from a hill
At thirty miles or more. The vision still
Lies in the eye, soft blue and far away:
The rain has washed the dust from April day;
Paint-brush and lupine lie against the ground;
The wind above the hill-top has the sound
Of distant water in unbroken sky;
Dark and precise the little steamers ply—
Firm in direction they seem not to stir.
That is illusion. The artificer
Of quiet, distance holds me in a vise
And holds the ocean steady to my eyes.

Once when I rounded Flattery, the sea
Hove its loose weight like sand to tangle me
Upon the washing deck, to crush the hull;
Subsiding, dragged flesh at the bone. The skull
Felt the retreating wash of dreaming hair.
Half drenched in dissolution, I lay bare.
I scarcely pulled myself erect; I came
Back slowly, slowly knew myself the same.
That was the ocean. From the ship we saw
Gray whales for miles: the long sweep of the jaw,
The blunt head plunging clean above the wave.
And one rose in a tent of sea and gave
A darkening shudder; water fell away;
The whale stood shining, and then sank in spray.

A landsman, I. The sea is but a sound.
I would be near it on a sandy mound,
And hear the steady rushing of the deep
While I lay stinging in the sand with sleep.
I have lived inland long. The land is numb.
It stands beneath the feet, and one may come
Walking securely, till the sea extends
Its limber margin, and precision ends.
By night a chaos of commingling power,
The whole Pacific hovers hour by hour.
The slow Pacific swell stirs on the sand,
Sleeping to sink away, withdrawing land,
Heaving and wrinkled in the moon, and blind;
Or gathers seaward, ebbing out of mind.

The Marriage

Incarnate for our marriage you appeared,
Flesh living in the spirit and endeared
By minor graces and slow sensual change.
Through every nerve we made our spirits range.
We fed our minds on every mortal thing:
The lacy fronds of carrots in the spring,
Their flesh sweet on the tongue, the salty wine
From bitter grapes, which gathered through the vine
The mineral drouth of autumn concentrate,
Wild spring in dream escaping, the debate
Of flesh and spirit on those vernal nights,
Its resolution in naive delights,
The young kids bleating softly in the rain—
All this to pass, not to return again.
And when I found your flesh did not resist,
It was the living spirit that I kissed,
It was the spirit's change in which I lay:
Thus, mind in mind we waited for the day.
When flesh shall fall away, and, falling, stand
Wrinkling with shadow over face and hand,
Still I shall meet you on the verge of dust
And know you as a faithful vestige must.
And, in commemoration of our lust,
May our heirs seal us in a single urn,
A single spirit never to return.

On a View of Pasadena from the Hills

From the high terrace porch I watch the dawn.
No light appears, though dark has mostly gone,
Sunk from the cold and monstrous stone. The hills
Lie naked but not light. The darkness spills
Down the remoter gulleys; pooled, will stay
Too low to melt, not yet alive with day.
Below the windows, the lawn, matted deep
Under its close-cropped tips with dewy sleep,
Gives off a faint hush, all its plushy swarm
Alive with coolness reaching to be warm.
Gray windows at my back, the massy frame
Dull with the blackness that has not a name;
But down below, the garden is still young,
Of five years' growth, perhaps, and terrace-hung,
Drop by slow drop of seeping concrete walls.
Such are the bastions of our pastorals!

Here are no palms! They once lined country ways,
Where old white houses glared down dusty days,
With small round towers, blunt-headed through small trees.
Those towers are now the hiving place of bees.
The palms were coarse; their leaves hung thick with dust;
The roads were muffled deep. But now deep rust
Has fastened on the wheels that labored then.
Peace to all such, and to all sleeping men!
I lived my childhood there, a passive dream
In the expanse of that recessive scheme.

Slow air, slow fire! O deep delay of Time!
That summer crater smoked like slaking lime,

The hills so dry, so dense the underbrush,
That where I pushed my way the giant hush
Was changed to soft explosion as the sage
Broke down to powdered ash, the sift of age,
And fell along my path, a shadowy rift.

On these rocks now no burning ashes drift;
Mowed lawn has crept along the granite bench;
The yellow blossoms of acacia drench
The dawn with pollen; and, with waxen green,
The long leaves of the eucalypti screen
The closer hills from view—lithe, tall, and fine,
And nobly clad with youth, they bend and shine.
The small dark pool, jutting with living rock,
Trembles at every atmospheric shock,
Blurred to its depth with the cold living ooze.
From cloudy caves, heavy with summer dews,
The shyest and most tremulous beings stir,
The pulsing of their fins a lucent blur,
That, like illusion, glances off the view.
The pulsing mouths, like metronomes, are true.

This is my father's house, no homestead here
That I shall live in, but a shining sphere
Of glass and glassy moments, frail surprise,
My father's phantasy of Paradise;
Which melts upon his death, which he attained
With loss of heart for every step he gained.
Too firmly gentle to displace the great,
He crystallized this vision somewhat late;
Forbidden now to climb the garden stair,
He views the terrace from a window chair.
His friends, hard shaken by some twenty years,
Tremble with palsy and with senile fears,

In their late middle age gone cold and gray.
Fine men, now broken. That the vision stay,
They spend astutely their depleted breath,
With tired ironic faces wait for death.

Below the garden the hills fold away.
Deep in the valley, a mist fine as spray,
Ready to shatter into spinning light,
Conceals the city at the edge of night.
The city, on the tremendous valley floor,
Draws its dream deeper for an instant more,
Superb on solid loam, and breathing deep,
Poised for a moment at the edge of sleep.

Cement roads mark the hills, wide, bending free
Of cliff and headland. Dropping toward the sea,
Through suburb after suburb, vast ravines
Swell to the summer drone of fine machines.
The driver, melting down the distance here,
May cast in flight the faint hoof of a deer
Or pass the faint head set perplexedly.
And man-made stone outgrows the living tree,
And at its rising, air is shaken, men
Are shattered, and the tremor swells again,
Extending to the naked salty shore,
Rank with the sea, which crumbles evermore.

The Journey

Snake River Country

I now remembered slowly how I came,
I, sometime living, sometime with a name,
Creeping by iron ways across the bare
Wastes of Wyoming, turning in despair,
Changing and turning, till the fall of night,
Then throbbing motionless with iron might.
Four days and nights! Small stations by the way,
Sunk far past midnight! Nothing one can say
Names the compassion they stir in the heart.
Obscure men shift and cry, and we depart.

And I remembered with the early sun
That foul-mouthed barber back in Pendleton,
The sprawling streets, the icy station bench,
The Round-up pennants, the latrinal stench.
These towns are cold by day, the flesh of vice
Raw and decisive, and the will precise;
At night the turbulence of drink and mud,
Blue glare of gas, the dances dripping blood,
Fists thudding murder in the shadowy air,
Exhausted whores, sunk to a changeless stare.
Alive in empty fact alone, extreme,
They make each fact a mortuary dream.

Once when the train paused in an empty place,
I met the unmoved landscape face to face;
Smoothing abysses that no stream could slake,
Deep in its black gulch crept the heavy Snake,
The sound diffused, and so intently firm,

It seemed the silence, having change nor term.
Beyond the river, gray volcanic stone
In rolling hills: the river moved alone.
And when we started, charged with mass, and slow,
We hung against it in an awful flow.

Thus I proceeded until early night,
And, when I read the station's name aright,
Descended—at the bidding of a word!
I slept the night out where the thought occurred,
Then rose to view the dwelling where I lay.
Outside, the bare land stretching far away;
The frame house, new, fortuitous, and bright,
Pointing the presence of the morning light;
A train's far screaming, clean as shining steel
Planing the distance for the gliding heel.
Through shrinking frost, autumnal grass uncurled,
In naked sunlight, on a naked world.

A Vision

Years had elapsed; the long room was the same.
At the far end, a log with drooping flame
Cast lengthening shadow. I was there alone,
A presence merely, like a shadow thrown,
Changing and growing dark with what I knew.
Above the roof, as if through a long flue,
The midnight wind poured steadily through pines.
I saw the trees flame thin, in watery lines.

Then, from my station in the empty air,
I saw them enter by the door; that pair
Opened and closed and watched each other move
With murderous eyes and gestures deep with love.
First came the Widow, but she had no face—
Naught but a shadow. At an earth-soaked pace
Her lover followed, weak with fear and lust.
And then I noticed there were years of dust
On floor and table, thought that in my day
No pines had been there. They sat down to play
At cards on a small table, and made tea,
And ate and played in silence. I could see
His lust come on him slowly, and his head
Fall on the table, but uncomforted
He feared to reach across to find her hand.
Deep in her veil I saw the features stand,
A deep jaw open; and a low iron laugh
Came from afar, a furious epigraph
To what I knew not in another place.
What evil was there in that woman's face!
He shrank in fear and told her of his love,

And she smiled coldly on him from above,
Stooped to a bundle lying by her side
And with a sodden tenderness untied
A severed head, gazed, and denied his plea.
He shuddered, heavy with lubricity.

There, steeped in the remote familiar gloom,
What were those demons doing in that room,
Their gestures aging, where the increasing shade
Stalked the dark flame that ever wearier played
As my receding memories left me dull?
My spirit now was but a shadowy hull.
Half-lost, I felt the Lover's shame my own.
I faced the Widow; we two were alone.

I saw the head and grasped it and struck root,
And then I rose, and with a steady foot,
I left her there, retarded in a dream.
Slowly I moved, like a directed beam.
My flesh fused with the cold flesh of the head;
My blood drew from me, from the neck flowed red,
A dark pulse on the darkness. The head stirred
Weakly beneath my fingers, and I heard
A whispered laughter, and the burden grew
In life and fury as my strength withdrew.
As if I labored up a flood of years,
I gathered heavy speed, drenched in arrears,
And limp to drowning, and I drove my flesh
Through the dark rooms adjacent to that mesh.
I was returning by the narrow hall;
Bound in my thought, jaw spread, I could not call.
And yet, with stride suspended in midair,
I fled more fast, yet more retarded there,

Swung backward by that laughter out of Hell,
Pealing at arm's length like an iron bell.

There in the darkest passage, where my feet
Fled fastest, he laughed loudest, and defeat
Was certain, for he held me in one place,
Fleeing immobile in an empty space,
I looked above me; on the stairway saw
The Widow, like a corpse. Fear drove my jaw
Wide open, and the tremor of that scream
Shattered my being like an empty dream.

Anacreontic

Peace! there is peace at last.
Deep in the Tuscan shade,
Swathed in the Grecian past,
Old Landor's bones are laid.

How many years have fled!
But o'er the sunken clay
Of the auguster dead
The centuries delay.

Come, write good verses, then!
That still, from age to age,
The eyes of able men
May settle on our page.

To a Young Writer

Achilles Holt, Stanford, 1930

Here for a few short years
Strengthen affections; meet,
Later, the dull arrears
Of age, and be discreet.

The angry blood burns low.
Some friend of lesser mind
Discerns you not; but so
Your solitude's defined.

Write little; do it well.
Your knowledge will be such,
At last, as to dispel
What moves you overmuch.

For My Father's Grave

Here lies one sweet of heart.
Stay! thou too must depart.
In silence set thy store—
These ashes speak no more.

By the Road to the Air-Base

The calloused grass lies hard
Against the cracking plain:
Life is a grayish stain;
The salt-marsh hems my yard.

Dry dikes rise hill on hill:
In sloughs of tidal slime
Shell-fish deposit lime,
Wild sea-fowl creep at will.

The highway, like a beach,
Turns whiter, shadowy, dry:
Loud, pale against the sky,
The bombing planes hold speech.

Yet fruit grows on the trees;
Here scholars pause to speak;
Through gardens bare and Greek,
I hear my neighbor's bees.

Elegy on a Young Airedale Bitch Lost Some Years Since in the Salt-Marsh

Low to the water's edge
You plunged; the tangled herb
Locked feet and mouth, a curb
Tough with the salty sedge.

Half dog and half a child,
Sprung from that roaming bitch,
You flung through dike and ditch,
Betrayed by what is wild.

The old dogs now are dead,
Tired with the hunt and cold,
Sunk in the earth and old.
But your bewildered head,

Led by what heron cry,
Lies by what tidal stream?—
Drenched with ancestral dream,
And cast ashore to dry.

Midas

Where he wandered, dream-enwound,
Brightness took the place of sound.
Shining plane and mass before:
Everywhere the sealëd door.
Children's unplacated grace
Met him with an empty face.
Mineral his limbs were grown:
Weight of being, not his own.
Ere he knew that he must die,
Ore had veinëd lip and eye:
Caught him scarcely looking back,
Startled at his golden track,
Immortalized the quickened shade
Of meaning by a moment made.

Sonnet to the Moon

Now every leaf, though colorless, burns bright
With disembodied and celestial light,
And drops without a movement or a sound
A pillar of darkness to the shifting ground.

The lucent, thin, and alcoholic flame
Runs in the stubble with a nervous aim,
But, when the eye pursues, will point with fire
Each single stubble-tip and strain no higher.

O triple goddess! Contemplate my plight!
Opacity, my fate! Change, my delight!
The yellow tom-cat, sunk in shifting fur,
Changes and dreams, a phosphorescent blur.

Sullen I wait, but still the vision shun.
Bodiless thoughts and thoughtless bodies run.

Before Disaster

Winter, 1932–3

Evening traffic homeward burns,
Swift and even on the turns,
Drifting weight in triple rows,
Fixed relation and repose.
This one edges out and by,
Inch by inch with steady eye.
But should error be increased,
Mass and moment are released;
Matter loosens, flooding blind,
Levels drivers to its kind.
   Ranks of nations thus descend,
Watchful to a stormy end.
By a moment's calm beguiled,
I have got a wife and child.
Fool and scoundrel guide the State.
Peace is whore to Greed and Hate.
Nowhere may I turn to flee:
Action is security.
Treading change with savage heel,
We must live or die by steel.

The Prince

The prince or statesman who would rise to power
Must rise through shallow trickery, and speak
The tongue of knavery, deceive the hour,
Use the corrupt, and still corrupt the weak.

And he who having power would serve the State,
Must now deceive corruption unto good,
By indirection strengthen love with hate,
Must love mankind with craft and hardihood:

Betray the witless unto wisdom, trick
Disaster to good luck, escape the gaze
Of all the pure at heart, each lunatic
Of innocence, who draws you to his daze:

And this frail balance to immortalize,
Stare publicly from death through marble eyes.

Phasellus Ille

After a poem by R. P. Blackmur

The dry wood strains, the small house stands its ground:
Jointed and tough, its sides shed off the storm.
And deep within, the heavy flame is warm,
Gold weight of peace on floor and chair enwound.
Wárm mínd, wárm héart, béam, bólt, and lóck,
You hold the love you took: and now, at length,
The mind and body, in new-wedded strength,
Toughen toward age, to brace against the shock.

Hold sure the course! the small house, like a boat,
Rides firm, intact, awaits the final blow.
Beneath, the current of impartial chance,
Disaster that strikes briefly and by rote,
The hazards of insane inheritance,
Láve our smóoth húll with what we little know.

Orpheus

In Memory of Hart Crane

Climbing from the Lethal dead,
Past the ruined waters' bed,
In the sleep his music cast
Tree and flesh and stone were fast—
As amid Dodona's wood
Wisdom never understood.

Till the shade his music won
Shuddered, by a pause undone—
Silence would not let her stay.
He could go one only way:
By the river, strong with grief,
Gave his flesh beyond belief.

Yet the fingers on the lyre
Spread like an avenging fire.
Crying loud, the immortal tongue,
From the empty body wrung,
Broken in a bloody dream,
Sang unmeaning down the stream.

On the Death of Senator Thomas J. Walsh

An old man more is gathered to the great.
   Singly, for conscience' sake he bent his brow:
He served that mathematic thing, the State,
   And with the great will be forgotten now.
The State is voiceless: only, we may write
   Singly our thanks for service past, and praise
The man whose purpose and remorseless sight
   Pursued corruption for its evil ways.

How sleep the great, the gentle, and the wise!
   Agëd and calm, they couch the wrinkled head.
Done with the wisdom that mankind devise,
   Humbly they render back the volume read—
Dwellers amid a peace that few surmise,
   Masters of quiet among all the dead.

Dedication for a Book of Criticism

To W. D. Briggs

He who learns may feed on lies:
He who understands is wise.
He who understands the great
Joins them in their own estate:
Grasping what they had to give,
Adds his strength that they may live.

Strong the scholar is to scan
What is permanent in man;
To detect his form and kind
And preserve the human mind;
By the type himself to guide,
Universal wisdom bide.

Heir of Linacre and More,
Guardian of Erasmus' store,
Careful knower of the best,
Bacon's scholar, Jonson's guest,
It was in your speaking lip
That I honored scholarship.

In the motions of your thought
I a plan and model sought;
My deficiencies but gauge
My own talents and the age;
What is good from you I took:
Then, in justice, take my book.

A Leave-Taking

I, who never kissed your head,
Lay these ashes in their bed;
That which I could do have done.
Now farewell, my newborn son.

On Teaching the Young

The young are quick of speech.
Grown middle-aged, I teach
Corrosion and distrust,
Exacting what I must.

A poem is what stands
When imperceptive hands,
Feeling, have gone astray.
It is what one should say.

Few minds will come to this.
The poet's only bliss
Is in cold certitude—
Laurel, archaic, rude.

Chiron

I, who taught Achilles, saw
Leap beyond me by its law,
By intrinsic law destroyed,
Genius in itself alloyed.

Dying scholar, dim with fact,
By the stallion body racked,
Studying my long defeat,
I have mastered Jove's deceit.

Now my head is bald and dried,
Past division simplified:
On the edge of naught I wait,
Magnitude inviolate.

Heracles

For Don Stanford

Eurystheus, trembling, called me to the throne,
Alcmena's son, heavy with thews and still.
He drove me on my fatal road alone:
I went, subservient to Hera's will.

For, when I had resisted, she had struck
Out of the sky and spun my wit: I slew
My children, quicker than a stroke of luck,
With motion lighter than my sinews knew.

Compelled down ways obscure with analogue
To force the Symbols of the Zodiac—
Bright Lion, Boundless Hydra, Fiery Dog—
I spread them on my arms as on a rack:

Spread them and broke them in the groaning wood,
And yet the Centaur stung me from afar,
His blood envenomed with the Hydra's blood:
Thence was I outcast from the earthy war.

Nessus the Centaur, with his wineskin full,
His branch and thyrsus, and his fleshy grip—
Her whom he could not force he yet could gull.
And she drank poison from his bearded lip.

Older than man, evil with age, is life:
Injustice, direst perfidy, my bane
Drove me to win my lover and my wife;
By love and justice I at last was slain.

The numbered Beings of the wheeling track
I carried singly to the empty throne,
And yet, when I had come exhausted back,
Was forced to wait without the gate alone.

Commanded thus to pause before the gate,
I felt from my hot breast the tremors pass,
White flame dissecting the corrupted State,
Eurystheus vibrant in his den of brass:

Vibrant with horror, though a jewelled king,
Lest, the heat mounting, madness turn my brain
For one dry moment, and the palace ring
With crystal terror ere I turn again.

This stayed me, too: my life was not my own,
But I my life's; a god I was, not man.
Grown Absolute, I slew my flesh and bone;
Timeless, I knew the Zodiac my span.

This was my grief, that out of grief I grew—
Translated as I was from earth at last,
For the sad pain that Deïanira knew.
Transmuted slowly in a fiery blast,

Perfect, and moving perfectly, I raid
Eternal silence to eternal ends:
And Deïanira, an imperfect shade,
Retreats in silence as my arc descends.

Alcmena

Now praise Alcmena for unchanging pride!
She sent her lover, when her brothers died,
To carry bloody death, where death was just;
The vengeance done, she yielded to his lust.
Zeus in the Theban halls her love besought:
To Zeus the greatest of his sons she brought:
The scion whom the god desired her for,
Alcides, Hero of Symbolic War.
She long outlived Alcides; when his son
Destroyed Eurystheus, and the feud was done,
She gouged the tyrant's eyes and cursed the head.
Then dense with age, she laid her on her bed.
But Zeus remembered the unbending dame,
Her giant maidenhood, the tireless frame,
That long had honored and had served him well,
And made her Rhadamanthus' queen in Hell.

Theseus: A Trilogy

For Henry Ramsey

I. The Wrath of Artemis

On the wet sand the queen emerged from forest,
Tall as a man, half naked, and at ease,
Leaned on her bow and eyed them. This, the priestess,
Who, with her savages, had harried Greece
From south to east, and now fought down from Thrace,
Her arrows cold as moonlight, and her flesh
Bright as her arrows, and her hatred still.
Heracles eyed the ground, and Theseus watched her.
Remote and thin as a bird-call over ice
From deep in the forest came the cry of her warriors,
Defiance from Artemis, the evasive daemon:
Hippolyta smiled, but Heracles moved softly
And seized her suddenly, bore her to the ship,
Bound her and left her vibrating like a deer,
Astounded beyond terror. And her women
Fell as they came, like water to dry earth,
An inundation of the living moon.

From out of the close hold of the nervous galley
She heard the shouting muffled in soft blood;
She heard it thinning quietly away.
And anger seized her; mind exceeded body,
Invoked divinity and rose to godhead:
She prayed the goddess to avenge the dead.
Then, in the doorway, blackened with maiden death,
Appeared the Attic conqueror in fulfillment.
Theseus, inexorable with love and war,

And ignorant with youth, begot upon her
A son, created in her shuddering fury,
To be born in Attica, the naked land.

In Attica, the naked land, she strode,
Brooding upon the secrets of the goddess,
Upon the wet bark of the Scythian forest,
The wet turf under bare foot, and the night
Blue with insistence of the staring eye.
The son, conceived in hatred, grew implacably,
Beyond her slow death, which he saw in passing,
Insolent, slender, effeminate, and chill,
His muscles made for running down the stag,
Dodging the boar, which Theseus would have broken,
Keeping step with the moon's shadows, changing
From thought to thought with an unchanging face.
He, judging Theseus from his narrow wisdom,
Yet judged him, and exiled him from his quiet,
The wrath of Artemis grown part of Theseus,
A man of moonlight and intensive calm.

II. Theseus and Ariadne

After the mossy night and the wet stone,
The grappling with the wet hair of the beast,
After the slow and careful fingering
Of the pale linen on the cold return,
Theseus emerged. Ariadne awaited him,
Her face half hidden with black hair and shame.

And Theseus spoke:
                    The Minotaur is dead.
Pasiphaë the white will sin no more:

The daughter of the moon, who bore this ghast
And dripping horror has been long at rest.
The sin of your blood I have extinguished; yet
Think not you will go quit. Your body is mine,
By all these tokens; and the taint of hell
Has eaten through my skin. Minos contrived
The trembling blackness of that hall of vision;
The prisoned fiend, your brother, beat me down,
I drew him after, and his blood burned through me,
Stinging more wildly than your body.

                            She:
My mother's sin has poisoned you, and I
Was poisoned long ago. We share this crime,
And I am yours, I know not to what end.
Minos' vengeance is buried in our two bodies.
You had me from Minos, should you prevail,
And Minos is the will of Zeus, withdraws not.
I am motionless in the scales of Justice.
We go now to your ship; the carven wood
Will glide in quiet from the rocks of Crete,
That bloodstained island of the gods, and we
Shall set our feet in peace on lesser isles.

So Theseus took her by the hand, boarded
The limber galley, and the foam distended
Coldly above the crash on rock. The boat,
Quick on the heavy tumult, scoured the inlets
And found that island where he slew her, yet
Escaped not, took her sister, her for whom
Poseidon betrayed him, when he slew his son.

III. The Old Age of Theseus

He gathered Phaedra, hard with childhood, small,
Shivering in arm and breast, into his arms.
He knew his age at last. Sin with this child
Was sin in solitude. Arms that had bound
The Heraclean bull, Phaea the sow,
That had fought side by side with Heracles
And beat their black way from the ice of Lethe,
Were hard with realized identity,
Beyond her comprehension, and he lay
Whole in the salty toughness of his age.

When he set foot in Attica, he found
Aegeus at rest, and he assumed the State.
Here were abstractions fitter for his years:
The calculation of corruption, thus
To balance evil against evil surely
And establish immitigable good.

                    He ruled
Hard in his certitude through Phaedra's death,
The betrayal of his son, that eccentricity
Of furious children. And he gathered up
The knowledge of his youth: the steady shame
Of tall Hippolyta; the calm of Aethra;
The quiet evil of the grave Medea;
The image of Pirithoüs in Hell,
Caught in the moving flesh among the shades—
Passion immovable!—the Orphic music
That swelled the measure of the Argo's oars
To a golden stride coëval with the Sun—
Gathered them slowly up and fed upon them,
Distilled from them the honey of calm wisdom—

The face of Ariadne dead, himself
Suddenly translated to another time.

Alone, he and the State. The State, established,
Exiled him into Scyros. Lycomedes,
The strange face of a king, was all that stood
Between him and himself. And Lycomedes,
The treacherous host, betrayed him to the State,
Which had betrayed him, to which he had been betrayed
By every movement of his flesh and spirit;
So cast him from the rock to solitude,
To the cold perfection of unending peace.

Socrates

For Clayton Stafford

We come now to the hemlock: this, the test
Of my daimonic promptings, of my long
Uncertain labor to discern the best,
To formulate forever what is wrong.

What is the city? What historic crux
Have we approached? Could but my skill endure,
The mind of Athens might surpass the flux,
When tongue and stone subside, her thought be sure.

If of my talking there should come a soul
Of tougher thought in richer phrase empearled,
Then were I sire and grandsire, scroll by scroll,
The vast foundation of a Western World.

While arguing amid the colonnades,
Tired in the noon-day by the badly taught,
Or resting, dubious, in the laurel shades,
I have impinged upon a firmer thought;

Have raised the Timeless up against the times;
The times, in turn, with this insensate cup,
Judge definition the most fierce of crimes;
The Timeless bids me drink the judgment up.

Thus are the times transmuted: understood,
A Timeless Form, comprising my estate.
Though what escapes them is my proper good,
Yet still would I be, so must they be, great.

Consistency gives quiet to the end.
My enemy is but a type of man,
And him whom I have changed, I call my friend.
The mind is formed. Dissuade it, he who can.

John Day, Frontiersman

Among the first and farthest! Elk and deer
Fell as your rifle rang in rocky caves;
There your lean shadow swept the still frontier,
Your eyes regarded the Columbia's waves.

Amid the stony winter, gray with care,
Hunted by savages from sleep to sleep
—Those patriots of darkness and despair!—
You climbed in solitude what rigid steep!

Broken at last by very force of frame,
By wintry hunger like a warrior's brand,
You died a madman. And now bears your name
A gentle river in a fertile land.

The eminence is gone that met your eye;
The winding savage, too, has sunk away.
Now, like a summer myth, the meadows lie,
Deep in the calm of silvan slow decay.

John Sutter

I was the patriarch of the shining land,
Of the blond summer and metallic grain;
Men vanished at the motion of my hand,
And when I beckoned they would come again.

The earth grew dense with grain at my desire;
The shade was deepened at the springs and streams;
Moving in dust that clung like pillared fire,
The gathering herds grew heavy in my dreams.

Across the mountains, naked from the heights,
Down to the valley broken settlers came,
And in my houses feasted through the nights,
Rebuilt their sinews and assumed a name.

In my clear rivers my own men discerned
The motive for the ruin and the crime—
Gold heavier than earth, a wealth unearned,
Loot, for two decades, from the heart of Time.

Metal, intrinsic value, deep and dense,
Preanimate, inimitable, still,
Real, but an evil with no human sense,
Dispersed the mind to concentrate the will.

Grained by alchemic change, the human kind
Turned from themselves to rivers and to rocks;
With dynamite broke metal unrefined;
Measured their moods by geologic shocks.

With knives they dug the metal out of stone;
Turned rivers back, for gold through ages piled,
Drove knives to hearts, and faced the gold alone;
Valley and river ruined and reviled;

Reviled and ruined me, my servant slew,
Strangled him from the figtree by my door.
When they had done what fury bade them do,
I was a cursing beggar, stripped and sore.

What end impersonal, what breathless age,
Incontinent of quiet and of years,
What calm catastrophe will yet assuage
This final drouth of penitential tears?

The California Oaks

Spreading and low, unwatered, concentrate
Of years of growth that thickens, not expands,
With leaves like mica and with roots that grate
Upon the deep foundations of these lands,
In your brown shadow, on your heavy loam
—Leaves shrinking to the whisper of decay—
What feet have come to roam,
                    what eyes to stay?
Your motion has o'ertaken what calm hands?

Quick as a sunbeam, when a bird divides
The lesser branches, on impassive ground,
Hwui-Shan, the ancient, for a moment glides,
Demure with wisdom, and without a sound;
Brown feet that come to meet him, quick and shy,
Move in the flesh, then, browner, dry to bone;
The brook-like shadows lie
                    where sun had shone;
Ceaseless, the dead leaves gather, mound on mound.

And where they gather, darkening the glade,
In hose and doublet, and with knotty beard,
Armed with the musket and the pirate's blade,
Stern as the silence by the savage feared,
Drake and his seamen pause to view the hills,
Measure the future with a steady gaze.
But when they go naught fills
                    the patient days;
The bay lies empty where the vessels cleared.

The Spaniard, learning caution from the trees,
Building his dwelling from the native clay,
Took native concubines: the blood of these
Calming his blood, he made a longer stay.
Longer, but yet recessive, for the change
Came on his sons and their sons to the end;
For peace may yet derange
                              and earth may bend
The ambitious mind to an archaic way.

Then the invasion! and the soil was turned,
The hidden waters drained, the valleys dried;
And whether fire or purer sunlight burned,
No matter! one by one the old oaks died.
Died or are dying! The archaic race—
Black oak, live oak, and valley oak—ere long
Must crumble on the place
                              which they made strong
And in the calm they guarded now abide.

On Rereading a Passage from John Muir

Seeking in vain to find the heroic brow,
The subject fitting for a native ode,
I turn from thinking, for there haunts me now
A wrinkled figure on a dusty road:
Climbing from road to path, from path to rock,
From rock to live oak, thence to mountain bay,
Through unmoved twilight, where the rifle's shock
Was half absorbed by leaves and drawn away,
Through mountain lilac, where the brown deer lay.

This was my childhood's revery: to be
Not one who seeks in nature his release
But one forever by the dripping tree,
Paradisaïc in his pristine peace.
I might have been this man: a knowing eye
Moving on leaf and bark, a quiet gauge
Of growing timber and of climbing fly,
A quiet hand to fix them on the page—
A gentle figure from a simpler age.

The Manzanita

Under the forest, where the day is dark
And air is motionless throughout the day,
Rooted in leaf-mould and in rotting bark,
This old arbutus gathers strength to stay.

Tall as a man, and taller, but more old,
This is no shrub of some few years, but hard
Its smooth unbending trunk, oh, hard and cold!
Of earth and age the stony proof and guard!

The skin is rose: yet infinitely thin,
It is a color only. What one tells
Of ancient wood and softly glinting skin
Is less than are the tiny waxen bells.

This life is not our life; nor for our wit
The sweetness of these shades; these are alone.
There is no wisdom here; seek not for it!
This is the shadow of the vast madrone.

Sir Gawaine and the Green Knight

Reptilian green the wrinkled throat,
Green as a bough of yew the beard;
He bent his head, and so I smote;
Then for a thought my vision cleared.

The head dropped clean; he rose and walked;
He fixed his fingers in the hair;
The head was unabashed and talked;
I understood what I must dare.

His flesh, cut down, arose and grew.
He bade me wait the season's round,
And then, when he had strength anew,
To meet him on his native ground.

The year declined; and in his keep
I passed in joy a thriving yule;
And whether waking or in sleep,
I lived in riot like a fool.

He beat the woods to bring me meat.
His lady, like a forest vine,
Grew in my arms; the growth was sweet;
And yet what thoughtless force was mine!

By practice and conviction formed,
With ancient stubbornness ingrained,
Although her body clung and swarmed,
My own identity remained.

Her beauty, lithe, unholy, pure,
Took shapes that I had never known;
And had I once been insecure,
Had grafted laurel in my bone.

And then, since I had kept the trust,
Had loved the lady, yet was true,
The knight withheld his giant thrust
And let me go with what I knew.

I left the green bark and the shade,
Where growth was rapid, thick, and still;
I found a road that men had made
And rested on a drying hill.

An October Nocturne

October 31st, 1936

The night was faint and sheer;
Immobile, road and dune.
Then, for a moment, clear,
A plane moved past the moon.

O spirit cool and frail,
Hung in the lunar fire!
Spun wire and brittle veil!
And trembling slowly higher!

Pure in each proven line!
The balance and the aim,
Half empty, half divine!
I saw how true you came.

Dissevered from your cause,
Your function was your goal.
Oblivious of my laws,
You made your calm patrol.

Much in Little

Amid the iris and the rose,
The honeysuckle and the bay,
The wild earth for a moment goes
In dust or weed another way.

Small though its corner be, the weed
Will yet intrude its creeping beard;
The harsh blade and the hairy seed
Recall the brutal earth we feared.

And if no water touch the dust
In some far corner, and one dare
To breathe upon it, one may trust
The spectre on the summer air:

The risen dust alive with fire,
The fire made visible, a blur
Interrate, the pervasive ire
Of foxtail and of hoarhound burr.

The Cremation

E.H.L.: 1866–1938

In Egypt, these five thousand years,
Men char with time, yet undispersed.
But we, whose mortal vision clears,
In one compact and final crash
In which a lifetime is reversed,
Sever the body from its ash.

The ash is but a little dust,
The body is eternal light.
And where is that which made you just?
Which gathered light about the bone
And moved the tongue, in earth's despite?
The powdered lime sinks back alone.

Thus you have left a fainter trace
Of what the spirit bore for hire
—No bony outline of a face!—
Than ages of the drying dead.
Once and for all you went through fire:
There is no footprint where you tread.

An Elegy

For the U.S.N. Dirigible, Macon

The noon is beautiful: the perfect wheel
Now glides on perfect surface with a sound
Earth has not heard before; the polished ground
Trembles and whispers under rushing steel.

The polished ground, and prehistoric air!
Metal now plummets upward and there sways,
A loosened pendulum for summer days,
Fixing the eyeball in a limpid stare.

There was one symbol in especial, one
Great form of thoughtless beauty that arose
Above the mountains, to foretell the close
Of this deception, at meridian.

Steel-gray the shadow, than a storm more vast!
Its crowding engines, rapid, disciplined,
Shook the great valley like a rising wind.
This image, now, is conjured from the past.

Wind in the wind! O form more light than cloud!
Storm amid storms! And by the storms dispersed!
The brain-drawn metal rose until accursed
By its extension and the sky was loud!

Who will believe this thing in time to come?
I was a witness. I beheld the age
That seized upon a planet's heritage
Of steel and oil, the mind's viaticum:

Crowded the world with strong ingenious things,
Used the provision it could not replace,
To leave but Cretan myths, a sandy trace
Through the last stone age, for the pastoral kings.

Time and the Garden

The spring has darkened with activity.
The future gathers in vine, bush, and tree:
Persimmon, walnut, loquat, fig, and grape,
Degrees and kinds of color, taste, and shape.
These will advance in their due series, space
The season like a tranquil dwelling-place.
And yet excitement swells me, vein by vein:
I long to crowd the little garden, gain
Its sweetness in my hand and crush it small
And taste it in a moment, time and all!
These trees, whose slow growth measures off my years,
I would expand to greatness. No one hears,
And I am still retarded in duress!
And this is like that other restlessness
To seize the greatness not yet fairly earned,
One which the tougher poets have discerned—
Gascoigne, Ben Jonson, Greville, Raleigh, Donne,
Poets who wrote great poems, one by one,
And spaced by many years, each line an act
Through which few labor, which no men retract.
This passion is the scholar's heritage,
The imposition of a busy age,
The passion to condense from book to book
Unbroken wisdom in a single look,
Though we know well that when this fix the head,
The mind's immortal, but the man is dead.

A Prayer for My Son

"Tangled with earth all ways we move."
— Janet Lewis

Eternal Spirit, you
Whose will maintains the world,
Who thought and made it true;
The honey-suckle curled
Through the arbutus limb,
The leaves that move in air,
Are half akin to him
Whose conscious moving stare
Is drawn, yet stirs by will;
Whose little fingers bend,
Unbend, and then are still,
While the mind seeks an end.
At moments, like a vine,
He clambers through small boughs;
Then poised and half divine,
He waits with lifted brows.
To steep the mind in sense,
Yet never lose the aim,
Will make the world grow dense,
Yet by this way we came.
Earth and mind are not one,
But they are so entwined,
That this, my little son,
May yet one day go blind.
Eternal Spirit, you
Who guided Socrates,
Pity this small and new
Bright soul on hands and knees.

In Praise of California Wines

Amid these clear and windy hills
Heat gathers quickly and is gone;
Dust rises, moves, and briefly stills;
Our thought can scarcely pause thereon.

With pale bright leaf and shadowy stem,
Pellucid amid nervous dust,
By pre-Socratic stratagem,
Yet sagging with its weight of must,

The vineyard spreads beside the road
In repetition, point and line.
I sing, in this dry bright abode,
The praises of the native wine.

It yields the pleasure of the eye,
It charms the skin, it warms the heart;
When nights are cold and thoughts crowd high,
Then 'tis the solvent for our art.

When worn for sleep the head is dull,
When art has failed us, far behind,
Its sweet corruption fills the skull
Till we are happy to be blind.

So may I yet, as poets use,
My time being spent, and more to pay,
In this quick warmth the will diffuse,
In sunlight vanish quite away.

A Summer Commentary

When I was young, with sharper sense,
The farthest insect cry I heard
Could stay me; through the trees, intense,
I watched the hunter and the bird.

Where is the meaning that I found?
Or was it but a state of mind,
Some old penumbra of the ground,
In which to be but not to find?

Now summer grasses, brown with heat,
Have crowded sweetness through the air;
The very roadside dust is sweet;
Even the unshadowed earth is fair.

The soft voice of the nesting dove,
And the dove in soft erratic flight
Like a rapid hand within a glove,
Caress the silence and the light.

Amid the rubble, the fallen fruit,
Fermenting in its rich decay,
Smears brandy on the trampling boot
And sends it sweeter on its way.

On the Portrait of a Scholar
of the Italian Renaissance

The color, quick in fluid oil,
Affirms the flesh and lambent hair;
And darkness, in its fine recoil,
Confesses that the mind is there.

With heavy lip, with massive curls,
With wisdom weighted, strong and dense,
The flesh is luminous as pearls;
The eyes ingenuous but intense.

The face is noble; but the name
Is one that we shall scarcely hold.
This is a vision in a frame,
Defined and matted down with gold.

Our names, with his, are but the lees
Residual from this clear intent;
Our finely grained identities
Are but this golden sediment.

A Winter Evening

Near Alviso, California

The earth for miles is massed with wet:
Small tree and bush and hedge of briar
Have sunk from shape with help nor let
As rank confusion gathers higher.

Each little house beside the road,
In weedy field, with rotting fence,
Groans and subsides, a broken load
Dropped there by thwarted diligence.

And by a swollen ditch, a dog,
Mud-soaked and happy, in a daze
Works into rain as dark as fog,
And moves down coldly solvent ways.

Summer Noon: 1941

With visionary care
The mind imagines Hell,
Draws fine the sound of flame
Till one can scarcely tell
The nature, or the name,
Or what the thing is for:
   Past summer bough and cry,
The sky, distended, bare,
Now whispers like a shell
Of the increase of war.
   Thus will man reach an end:
In fear of his own will,
Yet moved where it may tend,
With mind and word grown still.
   The fieldmouse and the hare,
The small snake of the garden,
Whose little muscles harden,
Whose eyes now quickened stare,
Though driven by the sound
—Too small and free to pardon!—
Will repossess this ground.

To a Military Rifle

1942

The times come round again;
The private life is small;
And individual men
Are counted not at all.
Now life is general,
And the bewildered Muse,
Thinking what she has done,
Confronts the daily news.

Blunt emblem, you have won:
With carven stock unbroke,
With core of steel, with crash
Of mass, and fading smoke;
Your fire leaves little ash;
Your balance on the arm
Points whither you intend;
Your bolt is smooth with charm.
When other concepts end,
This concept, hard and pure,
Shapes every mind therefor.
The time is yours, be sure,
Old Hammerheel of War.

I cannot write your praise
When young men go to die;
Nor yet regret the ways
That ended with this hour.
The hour has come. And I,
Who alter nothing, pray

That men, surviving you,
May learn to do and say
The difficult and true,
True shape of death and power.

.

For the Opening of the William Dinsmore Briggs Room

Stanford University, May 7, 1942

Because our Being grows in mind,
And evil in imperfect thought,
And passion running undefined
May ruin what the masters taught;

Within the edge of war we meet
To dedicate this room to one
Who made his wisdom more complete
Than any save the great have done.

That in this room, men yet may reach,
By labor and wit's sullen shock,
The final certitude of speech
Which Hell itself cannot unlock.

At the Site of the Murphy Cabin

Donner Lake, California

Earth overflows with water, and the pines
Grow cold and wet and heavy from this land.
The mountains, dense with undiscovered mines,
Rise, violent with shadow, close at hand,
A menace closing down without designs.
Disordered time! A hundred years ago
Men ate their dead, where we walk as we planned,

And grew in evil we may never know.
The fine snow grays the mountains; in the ground
Pure ice grows veins among the grains of sand,
Tiny, determined, and without a sound,
Like evil shrunk too fine to understand:
But just beneath the eye, beyond the sense,
Exacting caution with its imminence.

Moonlight Alert

Los Altos, California, June 1943

The sirens, rising, woke me; and the night
Lay cold and windless; and the moon was bright,
Moonlight from sky to earth, untaught, unclaimed,
An icy nightmare of the brute unnamed.
This was hallucination. Scarlet flower
And yellow fruit hung colorless. That hour
No scent lay on the air. The siren scream
Took on the fixity of shallow dream.
In the dread sweetness I could see the fall,
Like petals sifting from a quiet wall,
Of yellow soldiers through indifferent air,
Falling to die in solitude. With care
I held this vision, thinking of young men
Whom I had known and should not see again,
Fixed in reality, as I in thought.
And I stood waiting, and encountered naught.

To the Holy Spirit

From a deserted graveyard in the Salinas Valley

Immeasurable haze:
The desert valley spreads
Up golden river-beds
As if in other days.
Trees rise and thin away,
And past the trees, the hills,
Pure line and shade of dust,
Bear witness to our wills:
We see them, for we must;
Calm in deceit, they stay.

High noon returns the mind
Upon its local fact:
Dry grass and sand; we find
No vision to distract.
Low in the summer heat,
Naming old graves, are stones
Pushed here and there, the seat
Of nothing, and the bones
Beneath are similar:
Relics of lonely men,
Brutal and aimless, then,
As now, irregular.

These are thy fallen sons,
Thou whom I try to reach.
Thou whom the quick eye shuns,
Thou dost elude my speech.
Yet when I go from sense

And trace thee down in thought,
I meet thee, then, intense,
And know thee as I ought.
But thou art mind alone,
And I, alas, am bound
Pure mind to flesh and bone,
And flesh and bone to ground.

These had no thought: at most
Dark faith and blinding earth.
Where is the trammeled ghost?
Was there another birth?
Only one certainty
Beside thine unfleshed eye,
Beside the spectral tree,
Can I discern: these die.
All of this stir of age,
Though it elude my sense
Into what heritage
I know not, seems to fall,
Quiet beyond recall,
Into irrelevance.

A Song in Passing

Where am I now? And what
Am I to say portends?
Death is but death, and not
The most obtuse of ends.

No matter how one leans
One yet fears not to know.
God knows what all this means!
The mortal mind is slow.

Eternity is here.
There is no other place.
The only thing I fear
Is the Almighty Face.

At the San Francisco Airport

To my daughter, 1954

This is the terminal: the light
Gives perfect vision, false and hard;
The metal glitters, deep and bright.
Great planes are waiting in the yard—
They are already in the night.

And you are here beside me, small,
Contained and fragile, and intent
On things that I but half recall—
Yet going whither you are bent.
I am the past, and that is all.

But you and I in part are one:
The frightened brain, the nervous will,
The knowledge of what must be done,
The passion to acquire the skill
To face that which you dare not shun.

The rain of matter upon sense
Destroys me momently. The score:
There comes what will come. The expense
Is what one thought, and something more—
One's being and intelligence.

This is the terminal, the break.
Beyond this point, on lines of air,
You take the way that you must take;
And I remain in light and stare—
In light, and nothing else, awake.

To Herbert Dean Meritt

*Professor of English Philology at Stanford University
on his retirement*

Deep in the Cretan cave,
Each golden artifact
Or work in stone or clay
In palace hall or grave
Somehow appeared to stay—
For all the scholar lacked.

But round the buried word
Is only rich decay;
The meanings fall away.
What was it that man heard?
With cool persistent tact
You form what men would say.

Bibliography of Yvor Winters's Books of Poetry

The Immobile Wind. Evanston, Ill.: Monroe Wheeler, 1921.

Diadems and Fagots. Translations from the Portuguese of Olavo Bilac by John Meem and from the French of Pierre de Ronsard by Yvor Winters. Santa Fe, N.M.: privately printed, [1921].

The Magpie's Shadow. Chicago: Musterbookhouse, 1922.

The Bare Hills. Boston: Four Seas, 1927.

The Proof. New York: Coward McCann, 1930.

The Journey and Other Poems. Ithaca, N.Y.: Dragon Press, 1931.

Before Disaster. Tryon, N.C.: Tryon Pamphlets, 1934.

Poems. Los Altos, Calif.: Gyroscope Press, 1940.

The Giant Weapon. New York: New Directions, 1943.

To the Holy Spirit. Illus. Nick Carter. The California Folios, no. 11. San Francisco: Book Club of California, 1947.

Three Poems. Cummington, Mass.: Cummington Press, 1950.

Collected Poems. Denver: Alan Swallow, 1952.

Collected Poems. Rev. ed. Denver: Alan Swallow, 1960.

Collected Poems. Rev. ed. London: Routledge and Kegan Paul, 1962.

The Early Poems of Yvor Winters 1920–1928. Chicago: Swallow Press, 1966.

The Collected Poems of Yvor Winters. Intro. Donald Davie. Manchester: Carcanet New Press, 1978.

The Collected Poems of Yvor Winters. Intro. Donald Davie. [Title thus on title page; both the dust jacket and spine of the book list *The Poetry of Yvor Winters.*] Athens, Ohio: Swallow Press, Ohio University Press, 1980.

The Uncollected Poems of Yvor Winters 1919–1928. Ed. R. L. Barth. Edgewood, Ky.: Barth, 1997.

The Uncollected Poems of Yvor Winters 1929–1957. Ed. R. L. Barth. Edgewood, Ky.: Barth, 1997.

Poetry Anthologies Edited

Twelve Poets of the Pacific. Norfolk, Conn.: New Directions, 1937.

Poets of the Pacific: Second Series. Stanford, Calif.: Stanford University Press, 1949.

Quest for Reality: An Anthology of Short Poems in English. Ed. with Kenneth Fields. Chicago: Swallow Press, 1969.

Notes

In the effort to keep my commentary minimal, I had to make decisions that, in some cases, probably seem arbitrary. The first thing I deleted was textual commentary, essentially a recording of all textual variants for the poems included in this edition. I also decided that the educated general reader required neither mythological nor much literary annotation. That is, more or less major figures like Erasmus, Sir Walter Raleigh, and Hart Crane are not mentioned in my notes. What I have annotated are quotations from antiquity, figures literary and otherwise to whom Winters addressed poems or for whom he wrote them, and the inevitable odds and ends. Much of the commentary, however, consists of Winters's own notes to his *Poems* and *Collected Poems*. Despite taking J. V. Cunningham to task for writing about his own poems, Winters, albeit on a smaller scale, did the same. There are other important sources of commentary I have not quoted, most notably his criticism and the introduction to *The Early Poems of Yvor Winters 1920–1928*. These works are readily available, as the *Poems* is not. There are also the introduction to *Before Disaster* and fugitive pieces like his letter to the editor of the *New Republic* interpreting "Sir Gawaine and the Green Knight." To the interested reader, I recommend Grosvenor Powell's *Yvor Winters: An Annotated Bibliography 1919–1982* (Scarecrow, 1983).

In the notes following, I have abbreviated *Poems (P), Collected Poems (CP),* and *The Early Poems of Yvor Winters 1920–1928 (EP).* I have also abbreviated Yvor Winters (Y.W.) throughout.

The Dedication

J. L.W. (b. 1899): Y.W.'s wife, the poet and fiction writer Janet Lewis. This poem, not subsequently in *CP,* was the dedication to *Before Disaster.*

Early Poems

The early poems, from "Two Songs of Advent" to "Simplex Munditiis," are, unless otherwise noted, taken from *EP.* Of his early poems Y.W. said:

The earliest poems vacillate between an attitude—it was hardly more than that—of solipsism and one of mystical pantheism; gradually the solipsism tended to disappear and the pantheism to blur into a more literal determinism. The [later poems; that is, those following "Simplex Munditiis"] are based on the ideas which I have expounded in my criticism during the past ten years. The trouble with the ideas back of the early poems is an obvious one: they offer no method for discrimination between experiences except as one seeks either for mere descriptive accuracy or for emotion merely intense or strange; so that the literary discipline becomes largely a technique of inducing and fixing a kind of verbal hallucination, of which the comprehensible motive is seriously imperfect. (*P*, [58])

See also notes to "Nocturne" and "The Goatherds" for a continuation of this discussion.

The Cold

In *The Bare Hills* (1927) poems are grouped and numbered in various ways. When Y.W. selected some of the poems from this book for inclusion in *CP*, he dropped the numerical designations, as I have done. However, it is worth pointing out that this poem and the three following formed a complete group in the original volume.

Digue Dondaine, Digue Dondon

The title of this poem is from a French marching song, *"Sur la route de Dijon,"* which exists in numerous versions. The opening lines of one version follow:

> *Sur la route de Dijon*
> *La belle digue dig*
> *La belle digue don. . . .*

> On the high road to Dijon,
> Hey bella-dig-a-dig,
> Hey bella dig-a-don. . . .

> (trans. Barbara Scott, *Folk Songs of France*
> [New York: Oak Publications, 1966])

The note accompanying the version from which I quote reads: "The tune (and the words) would brighten anybody's journey." Clearly, Y.W. uses the song ironically.

Nocturne

Continuing his discussion of the early poems, Y.W. writes:

> Nocturne is another good example of material cohering by virtue of feeling and rhythmic structure, and very little by virtue of intelligible theme. If a poem of this sort were to be regarded as a true portrait of a state of mind, it would indicate madness on the part of the author; it is, of course, the result of a literary method by means of which certain elements of consciousness are isolated arbitrarily, as by a sieve. Unfortunately, as a spiritual exercise, this sort of thing can hardly lead toward intelligence, and is likely to lead away from it; and as a form of art it suffers from the elimination of those elements without which greatness is impossible, though if the poet have skill and good fortune he may within certain limits achieve extraordinary, if imperfect, beauty in some such manner (P, [59]).

"Quod Tegit Omnia"

The title is from Ovid's *Metamorphoses* I. The full passage reads as follows:

> *Ante mare et terras et quod tegit omnia caelum*
> *unus erat toto naturae vultus in orbe,*
> *quem dixere chaos:* (lines 5–7)

> Before the sea was, and the lands, and the sky *that hangs over all,* the face of nature showed alike in her whole round, which state men have called chaos: (trans. Frank Justus Miller). My italics translate the phrase used by Winters.

10–15. The second verse paragraph seems to rely primarily on the second speech of Socrates in the *Phaedrus,* the image in Y.W.'s poem of the bird deriving from Plato's image of the winged soul. The image of soul-as-bird is a neo-platonic commonplace, but it is best to assume that Y.W. has some specific Platonic text in mind. 14. cord Apparently a reference to the doctrine of "attunement" with its image of the lyre elaborated in the *Phaedo.*

17. **Sine pondere** "[things] without weight [and the sense includes a pun: imponderable]" quotes Ovid, *Metamorphoses* 1.20.

Prayer beside a Lamp

The epigraph quotes Ovid, *Metamorphoses* 2, telling the story of Phaëton. The full passage reads as follows:

> *vasti quoque rector Olympi,*
> *qui fera terribili iaculator fulmina dextra,*
> *non agat hos currus:* (lines 60–62)

> *even the lord of great Olympus,* who hurls dread thunderbolts with his awful hand, *could not drive this chariot:* (trans. Frank Justus Miller). My italics translate the epigraph.

Demigod

Text taken from *The Uncollected Poems of Yvor Winters 1919–1928.*

The Goatherds

Of this poem Y.W. says, "The Goatherds is merely descriptive—even the sea-shells are geological relics—yet by a kind of superimposed intensity of mood it seems to claim some ulterior significance, and it once tempted a young reviewer to the most patient and elaborate elucidation which, I believe, I have ever seen" (*P,* [57–58]). By way of example, Y.W. compares the methods and subjects of "The Goatherds" and "Nocturne" with "Midas," "Sonnet to the Moon," and "Sir Gawaine and the Green Knight," to mention the poems included in this selection, and the reader should consult the notes accompanying those poems.

Simplex Munditiis

The title is from Horace, *Odes* 1.5: *"Cui flavam religas comam, / Simplex munditiis?"* (lines 4–5). "For whom do you, *plain in neatness,* braid your golden hair?" My italics translate the phrase.

To William Dinsmore Briggs Conducting His Seminar

William Dinsmore Briggs (d. 1941): scholar and teacher who had a profound impact on Y.W. See also "Dedication for a Book of Criticism" and "For the Opening of the William Dinsmore Briggs Room" below.

The Invaders

"The Invaders are the modern scientists, of whom I should not write in quite the same terms today" (*P*, [59]).

The Castle of Thorns

"In medieval romance, which is a refurbishing of ancient folklore, the Robber Knight appears commonly to represent Death. In taking his victim to the castle, which is normally surrounded by a wood of thorn, he must in some way cross or dive under water, which is the most ancient symbol of the barrier between the two worlds" (*P*, [59]).

The Last Visit

Henry Ahnefeldt (1862–1929): Y.W.'s uncle.

For Howard Baker

Howard Baker (1905–1990): poet, novelist, critic, and rancher; member of the *Gyroscope* group; included in *Twelve Poets of the Pacific*.

The Journey

Y.W. says this poem is concerned with "the pull against gravity, against earth and those determined by it, and against the qualities one shares with them; self-direction, self-organized out of chaos" (*P*, [60]).

A Vision

"The Widow is Evil, half sensual, half spiritual; the head, her beloved and coadjutor, is Death; the lover is one beguiled and overcome. The observer, at first distinct from the lover, becomes one with him: as one might form one's character, personal or poetic, on a dangerous model, and so be possessed and destroyed" (*P*, [59]).

To a Young Writer

Achilles Holt (1911–1993): poet and fiction writer; student of Y.W.; included in *Twelve Poets of the Pacific*. Winters thought highly of Holt. In addition to this poem and "Chiron" (see below), Y.W. dedicated "The Anniversary" (not included here) to him and paid tribute to Holt's scholarship in a note to "Herman Melville and The Problems of Moral Navigation": "In my remarks on the symbolism of *Moby Dick*, I am indebted for a good many details to an unpublished thesis by Achilles Holt, done at Stanford University. Mr. Holt examines the subject very minutely, and I have used only a small part of his material; his thesis ought to be published" (*In Defense of Reason*, 200). Holt's writing career ended relatively early with the onset of severe mental illness.

For My Father's Grave

Y.W.'s father was Harry Lewis Winters (1876–1931).

Midas

According to Y.W., this poem "deals with the progress of illusion" (*P*, [59]).

Sonnet to the Moon

This poem "deals with the de-intellectualized sensibility" (*P*, [59]).

Phasellus Ille

Both Y.W.'s and Blackmur's poems derive from Catullus 4, which I give in the original Latin and Charles Martin's contemporary verse translation, followed by Blackmur's poem. Y.W.'s poem is a fine one in any case, but what seems to me the truly brilliant stroke is the transformation of Catullus's "phaselus" and Blackmur's "little boat" into a house riding out a storm.

Both Blackmur and Y.W. misspell "phaselus." I have been unable to determine why, although misremembered quotations and corrupt texts offer two plausible reasons.

Phaselus ille quem videtis, hospites,
ait fuisse navium celerrimus,
neque ullius natantis impetum trabis
nequisse praeterire, sive palmulis
opus foret volare sive linteo.
Et hoc negat minacis Hadriatici
negare litus insulasve Cycladas
Rhodumque nobilem horridamque Thraciam
Propontida trucemve Ponticum sinum
(ubi iste post phaselus antea fuit
comata silva—nam Cytorio in iugo
loquente saepe sibilum edidit coma).
Amastri Pontica et Cytore buxifer,
tibi haec fuisse et esse cognitissima
ait phaselus, ultima ex origine
tuo stetisse dicit in cacumine,
tuo imbuisse palmulas in aequore;
et inde tot per impotentia freta
erum tulisse, laeva sive dextera
vocaret aura, sive utrumque Iuppiter
simul secundus incidisset in pedem;
neque ulla vota litoralibus deis
sibi esse facta, cum veniret a mari
novissime hunc ad usque limpidum lacum.
Sed haec prius fuere; nunc recondita
senet quiete seque dedicat tibi,
gemelle Castor et gemelle Castoris.

*   *   *   *   *   *

Closer, friends: this little yacht you see before you
says that in her day no ship afloat was swifter,
no craft cut water whose wake she wasn't able
to leave behind, no matter whether her oarblades
drove her along or she relied on her canvas!
The shoreline of the blustery Adriatic
won't deny it, nor will the Cycladic Islands,
nor glamourous Rhodes, no—not even the wild Thracian

sea of Marmora, nor the grim gulf of Pontus,
where in the past our future yacht resided
as a green forest on the heights of Cytorus,
and where she learned to lisp in leafy syllables.
Pontic Amastris, Cytorus of the boxwood,
this little beanpod says that her past & present
are well known to you; she's certain you remember
how life began for her, perched atop your summit,
and how she first dipped her new oars into your waters,
leaving you on her maiden voyage through stormy
seas with her master, heading straight as an arrow
no matter whether the wind was holding steady
from port or starboard or from both sides together.
Nor was it ever necessary to offer
vows to the gods because of her performance
on the open seas or these more tranquil waters.
Now her career is ended, and in her old age
retiring, she dedicates herself to you two,
Castor the twin & the twin brother of Castor.

(Trans. by Charles Martin, The Poems of Catullus
[Baltimore: Johns Hopkins University Press, 1990], 6)

     *   *   *   *   *   *

Phasellus Ille

This little boat you see, my friends, has not,
as once Catullus' pinnace could repeat,
a history of deep-sea peril sought;
for her no honoured peace, no earned retreat.
Too narrow for her length in beam, unstable
and unseaworthy, her strakes and transom leak;
although no landsman, even, would call her able,
I float her daily in our tidal creek.

I do not need the bluster and the wail
in this small boat, of perilous high seas
nor the blown salt smarting in my teeth;
if the tide lift and weigh me in his scale

I know, and feel in me the knowledge freeze,
how smooth the utter sea is, underneath.

(Poems of R. P. Blackmur [Princeton:
Princeton University Press, 1977], 43)

On the Death of Senator Thomas J. Walsh

Thomas J. Walsh (1859–1933): U.S. Democratic senator (1913–1933) from Montana; exposed Teapot Dome scandal (1923); headed subcommittee that investigated leasing of naval oil reserves in California and Wyoming, resulting in the exposure of corruption in obtaining the leases.

Dedication for a Book of Criticism

This poem is a tribute to W. D. Briggs (for Briggs, see "To William Dinsmore Briggs Conducting His Seminar" above) as scholar and Y.W.'s teacher. "Dedication for a Book of Criticism" first appeared in print in *Before Disaster* (1934); Y.W.'s first real book of criticism (excluding thesis, dissertation, and "The Testament of a Stone," a twenty-page essay occupying an entire issue of *Secession*), *Primitivism and Decadence* (1937), was still three years in the future. It is possible that Y.W. once intended to preface that book with the poem. As published, without the poem, *Primitivism and Decadence* was dedicated to Briggs "with profound admiration and a very deep sense of intellectual indebtedness."

Chiron

A semi-autobiographical poem with Y.W. as teacher and by way of a pun Achilles [Holt] as student.

Heracles

Y.W. included the following note, which is of value for noting the source of his particular treatment of Heracles: "Heracles is treated as a Sun-god, the particular statement used, being that of Anthon's Classical Dictionary. Allegorically, he is the artist, in hand to hand, or intuitive, combat with experience. The apotheosis of the artist in the finished work" (*P*, [60]). **Don**

Stanford (1913–1998): poet, critic, scholar, and retired editor of the *Southern Review;* student of Y.W.; included in *Twelve Poets of the Pacific.*

Alcmena

Alcmena is "the ethical will, verging on barbarity, in itself, but, when impregnated with genius, producing the artist" (*P,* [60]).

Theseus: A Trilogy

Henry Ramsey (1910–1989): career diplomat; student of Y.W. and member of the *Gyroscope* group; included in *Twelve Poets of the Pacific.* Theseus is "the man of action" (*P,* [60]).

Socrates

Clayton Stafford (1903–1981): businessman and poet closely associated with Winters; included in *Twelve Poets of the Pacific.* As Theseus is the man of action, Socrates is "the man of principle" (*P,* [60]).

John Day, Frontiersman

John Day (c. 1772–1812): Virginia hunter and trapper. Joined an expedition financed by John Jacob Astor to Astoria, Oregon (1811–1812) for capitalist (fur trade) purposes. Washington Irving writes of him in *Astoria,* which is likely the source (at the least, one source) for Y.W.'s poem.

John Sutter

John Sutter (1803–1880): Swiss pioneer settler in California. He received a land grant from Mexico that attracted many settlers. During California's revolt against Mexico, he sided with the United States. After California was annexed, he and his partner built a sawmill on land where gold was discovered. Prospectors squatted on his land and, in time, disputed his ownership. The United States Supreme Court found his claims invalid. He died with a small pension, his grievances against the United States ignored.

The California Oaks

"There is a brief account of Hwui-Shan on pages 24–5 of *A History of California: The Spanish Period*, by Charles Edward Chapman. Hwui-Shan was a Chinese Buddhist priest, who may have come to California in 499 A.D. According to Chapman, the story is found in Volume 231 of the great Chinese Encyclopedia and in other works, and has long been known to Chinese scholars. Chapman believes that there were other Chinese voyages to the west coast of North American at very early dates" (*CP*, 146).

On Rereading a Passage from John Muir

John Muir (1838–1914): American naturalist and author of numerous volumes. I have been unable to identify the passage on which Winters based his poem.

Sir Gawaine and the Green Knight

This poem "represents the conflict between two aspects of human nature—the conscious, or intelligible and the sub-human" (*P*, [59]).

The Cremation

E.H.L. (1866–1938): Edwin Herbert Lewis, poet, novelist, and teacher; father of Janet Lewis Winters.

An Elegy

U.S.N. Dirigible, Macon: In the 1930s the United States Navy purchased two dirigibles, the *Akron* and its sister ship, *Macon*. The *Macon* was stationed on the west coast, the *Akron* on the east. The *Macon* was completed in 1933 and lost at sea during a storm in 1935, the *Akron* already having been lost in a storm. Janet Lewis wrote a fine poem on the subject, too:

The Hangar at Sunnyvale: 1937

Above the marsh, a hollow monument,
Ribbed with aluminum, enormous tent
Sheeted with silver, set to face the gale
Of the steady wind that filled the clipper sail,
The hangar stands. With doors now buckled close
Against the summer wind, the empty house
Reserves a space shaped to the foundered dream.
The Macon, lost, moves with the ocean stream.

Level the marshes, far and low the hills.
The useless structure, firm on the ample sills,
Rises incredible to state again:
Thus massive was the vessel, built in vain.
For this one purpose the long sides were planned
To lines like those of downward pouring sand,
Time-sifting sand; but Time immobile, stayed,
In substance bound, in these bright walls delayed.

This housed the shape that plunged through stormy air.
Empty cocoon! Yet was the vision fair
That like a firm bright cloud moved from the arch,
Leaving this roof to try a heavenly march;
Impermanent, impractical, designed
To frame a paradox and strongly bind
The weight, the weightless in a living shape
To cruise the sky and round the cloudy Cape.

Less substance than a mathematic dream
Locked in the hollow keel and webbéd beam!
Of the ingenious mind the expensive pride,
The highest hope, the last invention tried!
And now the silver tent alone remains.
Slowly the memory of disaster wanes.
Still in the summer sun the bastions burn
Until the inordinate dream again return.

(*Poems Old and New* [Athens:
Ohio University Press/Swallow Press, 1981], 67)

A Prayer for My Son

The epigraph is from Janet Lewis's sonnet, "The Earth-Bound," line 13.

On the Portrait of a Scholar of the Italian Renaissance

As Janet Lewis recalls, this was the portrait of an unnamed scholar by an anonymous artist.

For the Opening of the William Dinsmore Briggs Room

The W. D. Briggs room is "a reading room for graduate students in English, established as a memorial to the late head of the Stanford English department" (*CP*, 131).

At the Site of the Murphy Cabin

Text taken from *The Uncollected Poems of Yvor Winters 1929–1957*.

Moonlight Alert

Y.W. attempted to enlist in the Army in 1943. Rejected for medical reasons, he was appointed (at his own request) as Citizens' Defense Corps Zone Warden for Los Altos.

To Herbert Dean Meritt

Herbert Dean Meritt (1904–1984): Philologist and longtime colleague of Y.W. at Stanford.

Index of Poem Titles and First Lines